# Monkeyface

*a memoir*

JUDITH PODELL

For Zoey and Hannah

When you're grown up, these essays will
introduce you to the grandmother who made you
chicken schnitzel (Oma Chicken)
and had a toy store in her house.

# *Acknowledgements*

Thank you to the many unnamed, but vividly remembered, people who provided the meat for my memories; I couldn't have written this without you. And to my long-gone family members and those still here, I hope I've done justice to our shared history.

A shout-out to Chris Weeks, who gave structure and order to my jumble of words, and lastly, to Russell Steven Powell, my editor, who believed in me from the start and pushed me to keep writing and to dig deeper, but in the nicest way possible.

# *Foreward*

Whurrhen I met Judith Podell, I liked her instantly. She'd enrolled in a creative nonfiction class I was teaching at Westport Writers' Workshop, online thanks to the pandemic. I was struck at first by her quips, which on the surface appeared as castaway zingers, but quickly revealed themselves to be incisive comments on just about everything. Judy trades in a particular form of honesty, the kind that doesn't sneak up on you, but it doesn't hit you in the face either. Rather, her honesty hovers in view, waiting for you to do something with it. And you *should* do something with it, if you're smart enough to listen. Honesty is what holds Judy's writing together. With each new essay, we are treated to a frank look at one person's life, as well as a strong suggestion to face and reflect on our own.

Of her love of cars, for example, Judy writes, "Even in winter, I love driving with the roof open, the heater blasting. I've been told it's very inefficient and wastes gas, but I don't care." And that's the rub of Judy's work—it's a perfect duality. She doesn't care, but she does. Both are true. Similarly, who among us hasn't thought "I hate/I love" all at once? Judy says of her sisters, "They made me crazy: the TV tuned to ESPN the entire time, arguing over minutia, fussing about what to eat and how to cook things... I loved those weekends. I would give anything to have those days again." We are prompted to wonder what of our past makes us both fume and pine.

Judy candidly explores life as the daughter of Jewish immigrants in 1940s and '50s New York, and emphasizes the cultural significance of being in a family where European roots remain underfoot. She deftly acknowledges the ways being Jewish, and experiencing anti-Semitism, have shaped her life. Moreover, she shows readers how being female in male-dominated environments have bound her life with barriers asking to be shattered (with a machete, as you will see). Judy learned to think and be bigger than the world expects.

There's a constant tension in this collection between wanting to fit in and being willing to stand out. At one point, Judy heads off anti-Semitic comments by telling strangers she's Jewish; later, moving to a new place, she looks for a local synagogue: "I didn't want to live somewhere and be the only Jew in town." To both blend and remain true to herself, she writes, "Most of the time, I am just the old lady who lives in the cool house on the corner and paints stuff." True to Judy's wit, she is most definitely not "just" anything.

That wit is trademark to Judy's writing, something I've always admired. (As a writing instructor, I find wit a difficult trait to teach.) Lines that don't seem funny on the face of it are, in fact, arrestingly hilarious. During a New York City blackout, she spots lights across the Hudson: "I realized that if New Jersey still existed, it wasn't the end of the world." She need not explain further; indeed, throughout the collection, Judy ends essays with one-liners that float for a moment before sinking in.

What also threads together the essays is the push-pull between the spoken and unspoken. Moments of being silenced—for making a request, for not liking something, for forwardness—are met in equal measure by moments of speaking out. The book is a way to speak out continuously, no holds barred, no cultural obstructions in the way, no one but Judy to set the rules. For Judy, the fraught relationships with her parents, sisters, friends, neighbors, bosses, first husband, long-time second husband, and sons, can be examined and reexamined—finally—at this unique moment in her life: "Now, I'm the only one left." She's got a single, singular voice, and she uses it.

While peering closely at family, friends, work, and culture, Judy reveals a lot about others. The best essayists, however, don't hide from themselves or their readers. Judy is willing to admit her greatest failures ("Revenge and spite are my default modes") while honoring her greatest comforts ("I love the Seder now. I imagine Jews around the world saying the same words and singing the same songs and I think, *We are still here*."). From summer camp to college, time on a kibbutz to a traveling sales job, a philandering first husband to a devoted second, religious doubt to the invisibility that too often accompanies age for a woman, Judy lays bare everything it is to be a human in this complicated, maddening, beautiful world.

*What's the point of reliving it all?* Judy wonders aloud. These pages are the point. The record of a life lived with fierce intelligence, curiosity, and love.

Suzanne Farrell Smith

# Contents

## West Side Girl

## All Grown Up

# Working Girl

# Friendship

# On My Own

# West Side Girl

# *Driving Fool*

My father drove a blue Cadillac (always a Cadillac, always blue) to and from our summer home on Long Island before the Long Island Expressway was built and the only road was Route 25 winding through small towns and open fields. I sat in the front seat along with my mother because I got car sick. My two older sisters sat in back. The car had bench seats, and you could cram three, sometimes four passengers, depending on their size, in front and back; there were no such things as seat belts.

Those trips were the start of my love affair with cars. The drive took more than two hours. To stop our sibling squabbles, my mother would make us sing. A new immigrant, she favored American folksongs: "You Are My Sunshine," "Sweet Betsy from Pike,"

"Red River Valley," and others that I can't remember. The passengers (my parents, both my sisters, and sometimes Bridie, our Irish nanny who taught me songs, like, "Who Put the Overalls in Mrs. Murphy's Chowder"), are long gone and no one can fill in the empty spaces.

I must have outgrown the nausea because my strongest memory is being seated behind my father, leaning my forehead against the window, pretending I was astride a horse galloping alongside, jumping over the lines of tar that ran perpendicular to the highway creating bumps in the road as we drove over them.

It was in the Cadillac that I learned to drive. When I could reach the pedals, my father let me drive back and forth in the summer house driveway, an exercise that frequently ended with the car resting against the bordering hedge and me crawling out the passenger door.

In college, a boy, whose name I don't recall, taught me to drive a stick shift in his old, beat-up station wagon. Never saying a word at my incompetence, he'd place his arm over the back of my seat and brace himself as I took my eyes off the road to stare at my feet while trying to make shifting, steering, clutch, and gas pedal all work together. Fortunately, I always stalled out before I hit anything.

I think only old people now remember how to drive a "standard."

Cars, especially convertibles, were places to make out in, to escape from parents, to show off (like turning off the headlights while going 60 mph) and other foolishness; that I survived all of that is remarkable.

A black Geo Prizm was my first car with a sunroof; I've never had a car since without one. For most of the summer and even in winter, I love driving with the roof open, the heater blasting. I've been told it's very inefficient and wastes gas, but I don't care.

My husband, David, once bought me a set of magnetic decals of red and yellow flames for my birthday that I put on the side front fenders of the Prizm (and subsequently transferred to later cars). I drove with my seat tilted way back. David said I was channeling my inner teenage punk.

Once, while driving to a painting class in Rhode Island, I was stopped by a state trooper. Walking to the driver's side of the car, the trooper leaned into my window and asked, "Whose car is this?"

Mine, I said, and why did he ask? "There are flames on the hood," he said.

I babbled about always wanting flames, that they were my husband's birthday gift. When I paused for breath, he stood silently for a few seconds, told me to slow down, and walked away.

In the 60-plus years I've been behind the wheel, not much has changed about me and my love affair with driving. My current Beemer may be my last car. Maybe I can be buried in it. Seat way back, sunroof open. Must add that to my will.

# Sisters, Sisters

I thought the death of my husband was the worst thing that could ever happen to me. I am discovering that the loss of both my sisters is equally unsettling. Since 2014, I've been an only child as by then, both my sisters had died within 18 months of each other.

Eva, the eldest, died from bladder cancer. Wiry, fierce, and seemingly indomitable, it was shocking how quickly and totally it consumed her. On her deathbed she looked like a newly hatched chick, all head, bones, and skin.

Ruthi had struggled for years from a massive stroke at age 50 which crippled one side of her body, her left hand frozen permanently into a claw; she named it Fred and joked it was an excellent paperweight. Twenty-plus years later, she developed acute myeloid leukemia and underwent a bone marrow transplant, which extended her life, but not its quality; she died mercifully, not many months after Eva.

Both gone under very different circumstances but looking the same on death's edge. It's irrelevant that I couldn't spend more than two days in their company before they got on my nerves. What difference does it make if I pitied, disliked, or found irritating so much about them — they were the immutable elements of my childhood; always there, in the background, if not front and center of most memories. Without them, I am untethered.

———————

I was my mother's favorite; I looked most like her. The only one born in the United States, she joked that I was her American baby: plump and blond, sunny disposition. My sisters were both born in France. Their first memories were of fleeing Europe before war was declared. They were dark-haired, anxious, sallow-skinned.

Eva was the son my father never had. Slim and athletic, her face was unattractive with a long nose that shadowed her upper lip in family photos. It made her pugnacious and belligerent, quick to take offense. When she was 18, she had rhinoplasty, a "nose job," a procedure common among upper-middleclass Jewish girls at that time. But whereas girls usually requested and received tiny, upturned noses, Eva wanted only that the part of her nose that drooped at the tip be removed. The surgery did little to change her face but dramatically affected her personality. She became a much nicer person.

She was the family jock, excelling in every sport she tried, finally settling on tennis, which she built a life around. Growing up, Eva had her own room and while she frequently fought with Ruthi (I'm talking words and fists), she basically ignored me for most of my childhood.

After she married, she moved away from the New York area where both Ruthi and I lived and settled in Virginia. She was not part of my life until many years later when her granddaughter's bat mitzvah brought us all together. After that, we started a new tradition, where I would come visit annually, making the long train ride from Connecticut for a few days each June. She would take me to the art museum (Richmond has a very impressive one), the botanical garden, we'd go out to dinner. She'd fuss over food I liked, I planted garden pots for her, we picked out colors together and she let me paint several rooms in her house.

Ruthi, the middle child, was nobody's favorite. Two-and-a-half years older than I, she unfortunately resembled one of my father's sisters, the one he didn't like. She struggled to find her place and so, became "the smart daughter." She read every volume of the *Encyclopedia Britannica*, the 20-plus volumes that occupied a whole bookshelf in the bedroom that we shared. She had an explosive temper, disliked me, and made no effort to hide her feelings. I would try to stay awake until she was asleep as I feared she would kill me in the night, a not unreasonable fear as I was adept at provoking her and pushing her buttons and then hiding out to avoid being attacked.

As adults, Ruthi and I were estranged after a blowout fight at a family gathering at my home. I had spoken sharply to my mother, who was bossing everyone around, including me. When I told her to stop, my sister stepped in demanding, "Don't talk to my mother that way!" I told her it was my house and I'd talk to OUR mother anyway I wanted and if Ruthi didn't like it, she could leave. And she did, in a huff.

After that, we went our own ways and didn't speak for several years. That changed after her stroke. Her husband called me in the middle of the night to tell me she was in the hospital. I drove down and found her lying on a gurney in the hospital corridor, one side of her face badly contorted and drooping. I leaned close and said, "You know, if you really didn't want to go visit Mother today, you could have just said so." She laughed a one-sided guffaw, and I stayed with her until morning and then drove to New York to tell our mother. We spent a lot of time together after that. While physically she never really recovered, our relationship became stronger and remained so until her death.

We were "The Passweg Girls." We had a certain arrogance, we were not the prettiest — not by a long shot — but we were smart, clever, cocky. We were very different in personalities and looks, but all three of us had an attitude, a toughness that said, "don't mess with us." When I went through a divorce from my first husband (a story for another day), they were my staunchest allies.

My happiest memories are of the annual long fall weekend the three of us would spend together, without spouses or children, in North Carolina at Ruthi's beach home. They made me crazy: the TV tuned to ESPN the entire time, arguing over minutia, fussing about what to eat and how to cook things ... I loved those weekends. I would give anything to have those days again.

Now, I'm the only one left. I think of them often, regretting the missed opportunities, the wasted energy, the fights, and hurtful words. Mostly I remember the camaraderie, the laughter, the moments we had each other's backs, the love.

# *Teenage Angst*

I was a complicated teenager. Perhaps that's redundant, as the word itself embodies all the mixed emotions and raging hormones of youth.

Until then, I had been the "good daughter," sunny, obedient, compliant. Not anymore.

Dinner with the whole family, my father at the head of the table, my sisters on his right, my mother at the other end, and me, on her right. I am 12 or 13. Some criticism is given, I throw down my napkin and retreat in tears to my room. This happens regularly.

I'm a late bloomer; other classmates wear bras before me. After begging my mother, I finally get a small wisp of white cotton that serves no function as there is so little to support. I am thrilled and embarrassed and wear a T-shirt under my blouse so no one will see the straps.

The other girls make fun of me because I don't tweeze my eyebrows or shave my legs. I want to be like them, dress like them, something my mother can't understand. "Be yourself!" she says.

I stare in the mirror and despair at my flat chest. I take a charcoal stick and draw a line on my chest to give myself cleavage. Every pimple is epic. I didn't suffer the corrosive landscape of acne that tormented other teens. Instead, a single pustule emerges, grows, and festers until it bursts and eventually disappears (that is, if I don't pick at it and make it worse). I slather "pancake" makeup, a coating of color housed in a round compact, all over my face to obscure those zits and flaws; my face becomes a smooth mask of orange.

And then there's my period. My mother has left a book in my bedroom, *The Stork Didn't Bring You*, which I read multiple times until I know it practically by heart. My only memory is drawings of the fallopian tubes, resembling a Georgia O'Keefe bleached steer skull. I use sanitary pads which are enormous and held in a garter-like arrangement that settles on my hips like a gunslinger's belt. I am in constant anxiety that blood will leak through, or worse, that someone can see the outline of the pad through my clothing.

Were there dispensers in the girls' bathroom at school? I don't remember. I carry extra pads in my shoulder bag or in an emergency run the two blocks home to change. That year at summer camp, Ruthi introduces me to tampons. I don't understand her instructions and waddle awkwardly, legs spread wide in pain until I learn how to insert them properly.

At 14, I start smoking. A filthy habit, one that tastes bad and makes my body smell even worse. It will take me 35 years to quit.

In high school during lunch period, I hang out on the school steps with older kids, who share their cigarettes. It feels grown up and sophisticated, that's reason enough. I am watchful, as sometimes my mother drives by the school when she takes her car from the garage around the corner.

There is a small pharmacy a few blocks away. It serves food, and a gaggle of classmates go regularly after school and sit at the counter. I imagine myself having a cup of coffee and a cigarette, a woman of the world. Only coffee makes me gag, so I settle for a cigarette and a chocolate egg-cream; not the look I was going for.

I attend class parties at someone's apartment. A classmate disappears into a bedroom with a boy, and then another. We play "spin the bottle," which involves kissing the person the bottle points to. Other times the rules change, and you would have to remove an item of clothing each time the bottle points at you.

Some girls took off their blouses or bras, I am wary and never play past shoes, socks, or belt.

Pranks are more common than these sexual games. Calling random numbers in the phone book and telling the party on the other end their refrigerator is running, or asking for Harry, after 10 such calls, call and say ... "Hi, this is Harry, any messages?" before hanging up. A rotary phone with a dial was the instrument of harassment; no consequences as there was no such thing as caller ID or call blocking.

A classmate invites me out on a date. He's the most mature of all the boys (he grew his own beard for a part in *Caesar and Cleopatra*; all the other boys had theirs drawn on). He takes me to a restaurant in the Hotel Lexington, a first for me. I scan the prices and eat very little — I want to appear ladylike. When returning home after an awkward goodnight kiss, I devour half a roasted chicken.

Today, I remember that younger me with bemusement. I have outgrown most of the behaviors that marked my adolescence. I've learned better, more subtle ways of masking my anxieties and fears. My public persona is of a confident woman with a loud voice and strong opinions.

That insecure, wanting-to-fit-in girl is buried deep, no longer visible, but she's in there.

# What's in a Name?

Somewhere around age 50, I decided that the name "Judy" didn't fit me. The diminutive for "Judith" seemed ... too cute, not serious enough for a grown woman. I think it's the "y" ending that does it. Think about it: Betty, Johnny, Patty, Billy, Debby. Not much gravitas there.

My French mother had wanted to name me, her first American baby, Françoise, after her homeland. Having given her two other daughters Biblical names, she chose Judith as my middle name. It comes from the story of a beautiful widow whose village was besieged by the Assyrians and how she seduced and then murdered their general, Holofernes, by cutting off his head, thus saving the Jewish people. A gruesome tale, but as I got older, I came to appreciate my namesake's courage and determination; certainly, a ballsy woman, and thus a name worth growing into.

Unfortunately, the hospital bureaucrat who completed my paperwork wasn't paying attention. Perhaps in an attempt to Americanize my name, or maybe just plain sloppiness, Françoise became Frances, the order was reversed, and I became Judith Frances, and that was that. I am actually grateful to that nameless clerk; if not for that error, my sister Ruth would forever have branded me, "Fanny," or "Frances the Talking Mule," after a TV show featuring a donkey.

My oldest sister was named Eva Xenia. Her middle name was in honor of my father's childhood nurse-maid. Her nickname was "Hami," which supposedly means "little lamb," although I can find no such reference in German, French, or Polish. Trust me when I say that there never was a name and a person so mismatched. It was only okay to call her that in the privacy of our home; if you used it in front of school friends or boys, there was hell to pay.

My second sister, four years younger than Eva, was Ruth Salome (try living with that moniker). I don't think she ever told anyone her middle name.

In the private school I attended, there were two Judys. To distinguish between us, the other girl was known as Judy M, I was Judy P. This was considered hilarious by the adolescent boys in my class, which is why I never ran for any leadership positions so I wouldn't have to endure hearing, "all those for Judy P" when a vote was called, which would have the boys rolling on the floor in stitches.

One of my son's classmates was named "Marlin Blue," which of course appeared on any list as "Blue Marlin." What were his parents thinking?

Do names shape who we become? Would I be a different person if I had been named Natasha or Shoshanna, both names I always liked? Perhaps. I'll never know. Today, many people change their names for gender identity reasons. Marilyn becomes Mitch, Joe, Joanna. Whatever the reason, the name you use is how you present yourself to the world.

Today I sign my name as Judith, not Judy. As Judith, I stand taller, speak more confidently, even if most people still call me Judy.

# *Benno*

My father's name was Benzion, "Son of Zion," but family and friends all called him Benno. Obituary tributes to him in the *New York Times* referred to him as Ben T. Passweg. Non-Jewish colleagues called him Ben and thought it was short for Benjamin.

As the youngest of his three daughters, he and I had a special relationship. We shared a love of fish — and fishing. He kept a boat in Long Island, near the Jones Inlet, and I was the daughter who went with him, starting when I was about 10.

He'd wake me at four a.m. and we'd drive to the South Fork of Long Island, where his boat was moored. Gustav, his oldest and closest friend, came as well. He and his wife, Clara, who was my mother's best friend, would stay with us on the weekends.

They had no children and were like family. The boat was my father's, but it was Gustav who took the navigation courses and knew how to repair the engines.

We ate enormous breakfasts at a local diner and then headed out in the early dawn after bluefish. I never got seasick. I loved everything about those days, the breakfast, the chill of the morning, the rocking of the boat, the mist that hung over the water until the sun was higher in the sky.

We fished with live bait, and I learned to bait my own hook, and to be patient and wait for the tiny tugs on the line that meant a fish was nibbling. Then, just at the right moment, jerk the rod up and quickly start reeling in my catch.

Our fondness for fish extended to an enormous aquarium in our apartment. This tank on a metal stand was about four feet long and two feet high and stood in the living room between the two large windows that faced Central Park. It was my father's pride and joy. Ours was a "community tank," with a wide variety of fish: guppies, black mollies, various barbs, angelfish, neon tetras, zebrafish, and gouramis. Also "street cleaners," the several kinds of catfish that stayed at the bottom of the tank and snuffled their way like vacuums across the gravel.

I don't remember exactly when, but at a holiday family get-together, a young cousin tipped a chair back into the aquarium and shattered the glass, sending 150 gallons of water and fish crashing onto the floor. Weeks later, we continued finding desiccated carcasses on the oriental carpet. We got another, much smaller tank, that was housed in my sister's and my bedroom. My father never spoke to that cousin again.

———————

My father was unfaithful to my mother. I didn't know that when I was young, but I remember the fights, late at night, usually in German, which I didn't understand. Children see and understand more than adults think; they observe people and their interactions. Between my father and certain women there were signs of intimacy: glances, touches. There was a buyer for his shoe company, who I met when I worked for him in his office in the Empire State Building on summer breaks from school. And there were others, including a woman, the mother of my oldest sister's schoolmate, who my mother considered a close friend. That affair ended their friendship.

My father was a part-time Dad. He split the work week between our Manhattan apartment and eastern Pennsylvania, where his three shoe factories were located. When he would arrive home to our apartment after days away, my mother insisted that we girls sat with him while he ate dinner even though it was long after we'd eaten.

He lived large. He would create endless pranks and schemes, along with Gustav, normally a dour, humorless man. Once, after a meal at a maiden aunt's apartment, the two men offered to do the dishes, and then proceeded to break every plate, as they tossed them back and forth, letting them drop from their hands. The wives shrieked at them; my aunt was in hysterics. Turns out they had bought a set of cheap dishes and those were what they smashed.

Another typical lark occurred at a dinner party with friends of a colleague. Apparently, the conversation was stiff and stilted, until when dessert was served — a chocolate mousse with whipped cream. Whereupon my father took the bowl of whipped cream, stood behind Gustav's chair, draped his dinner napkin around his neck and tilting his head back, proceeded to lather and shave him with a butter knife. Apparently the party relaxed considerably after that, and a good time was had by all.

I wish I could have been there!

He laughed a lot and told me my first dirty joke (see *Make 'em Laugh*).

My father died the night of the first major blackout in New York City in 1965. He was 59 years old.

Since then, there have been many such blackouts, but that first one was terrifying. My father had been ill at home for several days, and the doctor decided the day before to move him to the hospital. My mother was staying at a close friend's apartment near the hospital. We girls were alone at home.

It was dusk. I was standing, looking out the living room windows and suddenly the room and everything outside the window went completely dark. Was it an invasion? The beginning of a war? Something terrible must be happening. But then, I saw that in the west, the New Jersey skyline twinkled with lights and I realized that if New Jersey still existed, it wasn't the end of the world.

My sister Ruthi, with a bad knee, couldn't manage the stairs, so we left her, all alone, in the dark, unable to communicate with anyone, while somehow my eldest sister and I walked down the 26 flights of stairs to the building's garage, found our car and drove across the completely dark city — no streetlights, or working traffic signals to the lit-up hospital, where emergency generators kept essential services and equipment working. The last time I saw my father his skin was yellow, his breathing labored, and he had a wild-eyed stare. The rest is a blur. Sleeping on the floor of the friend's apartment, the call from the hospital early the next morning, my mother's wails.

Am I like him? When we are young, we think we will choose who to be when we grow up. So much of who we are seems baked in at birth.

I think I have his sunny disposition and optimism. I hope I have his people skills, his charm, and humor, his exuberance and playfulness. My youngest son, whose middle name is Benzion, has inherited those gifts and reminds me of him more and more every day.

# Like Mother, Like Daughter

Of all the roles I've filled, the most important one, mother, is the one I did least well.

I come by my incompetence honestly; my mother was a miserable role model. She grew up in France, one of ten children of an alcoholic father and an overburdened mother. She went to school until she was 13, and then to work. Narcissistic, needy, she was a leaky bucket — never getting enough love — not from her parents, not from her husband. She was a much better friend than mother. It has only recently occurred to me that three of her closest friends in America had no children. I wonder if that impacted her mothering — she had no one to advise her, only her own experience, which was dismal.

I am so like her.

My sharp tongue, and I fear, my even more vindictive spirit. I have her toughness and her creative gifts (that seem to run in her family), and her loyalty. While inadequate as a mother, she was a great friend; I, too, have lifelong friends. I also have her unforgiving nature, her ability to hold a lifetime grudge. Revenge and spite are my default modes. Are my character flaws all her fault? And what good does that do me to blame her now, dead these many years?

I try to atone for my past inadequacies by being a better grandmother. I remind myself that everyone had a mother, and most children overcome the shortcomings of their parents. But it weighs on me to this day.

She called me "monkeyface," an affectionate sobriquet. The one in looks, in temperament, in creativity, who would fulfill all her hopes and dreams. I acquiesced until my teens. Then everything changed. I stopped being the obedient, compliant daughter. When we fought, my mother's punishment was to stop talking to me. She simply ignored me, would act as if I weren't at the table or in the room. My father would step in and tell me to apologize to her. I argued that she was in the wrong, I made my case, mustered cogent and compelling evidence, and he responded,

"She's your mother, apologize." I did, but the sting of the injustice of it never went away.

When I was in college, I became pregnant by an older man, my first lover. In the early '60s, this was a big deal. Abortions were illegal, and I spent sleepless nights panicked and scared, trying to figure out what to do. Flashes of memory. A train ride alone ... where had I gone? There was a man, he injects me with an abortifacient. Then the long ride home, surrounded by college boys on school break, joking and horsing around while I lean against the window, nauseous and in pain. Back home, I lay curled up in my bed, vomiting. Someone calls an ambulance. A family friend, a childless woman, who lives in our building, rides with me in an ambulance, she is stroking my hair. That's all I remember. My mother had retreated to her bedroom and refused to speak to me. Was she ashamed of me? Angry, disappointed? We never spoke about it.

I think that's when I stopped loving my mother. Pity, empathy, yes. But not love. I don't think I ever really forgave her; holding a grudge — another trait we shared in common.

I remained a dutiful daughter. After my father's death, I encouraged her to go to college, a journey that brought her much happiness. She began having strokes. They increased in frequency and after the last major one, while she was still living independently, the ER doctor stated, "she can't live on her own, she needs to go into a nursing home." She begged me not to do that — a move my sisters were prepared to do. I talked them out of it, and we moved her into the assisted living apartment she had just purchased and hired 24-hour care. That's where she died, not long after, surrounded by her memories, paintings, and sculptures, as she had wished.

With the perspective of time, I see my failures clearly, cringing at the memories. I also see her more fully. She was tough, brave, and persistent. I am her daughter.

# *Puzzles*

I started doing jigsaw puzzles when I was 11 years old. That summer, I was diagnosed with poliomyelitis, in what became the worst polio epidemic in history. We were at our summer house on Long Island, my mother had dropped us three girls off in town at the movie theater to see Bing Crosby and Bob Hope in *Road to Bali.*

After the movie I remember we went for ice cream before we were picked up and I, for once, wasn't hungry, but just wanted to go home. I must have run a fever, because a doctor came to the house (those were the days!) who said it was polio. My mother and I stayed as my father took my sisters back to New York City. She cared for me with the aid of a nurse who came several times a week. The treatment was applying hot compresses throughout the day. When I cried that they were too hot, my mother would reply, "they're hotter in the hospital," and I shut my mouth.

I was confined upstairs to my parents' bed. The only thing I remember besides the hot pack treatments is sleeping and doing jigsaw puzzles. There was little else I could do. I had a large board which held the assembled pieces. Intricate and beautiful, they were cut out of wood and the finished puzzle could hold together when held aloft by two corners. The images were classic paintings. After I completed a puzzle, I would do it again, only this time, turned over, with no image, assembling it from the shapes alone.

Eventually we returned to the city (weeks, months later?), and I went back to school, a small four-story building two blocks from our apartment building. I was weak and needed to take the elevator up to our classroom and down to the lunchroom while everyone else walked the stairs. Early in my return, I remember an incident when I got on the elevator. As the door closed, I could hear my classmates complaining angrily, "Why does she get to ride?" Apparently, the teacher told them of my condition, for when I got off, shamefaced peers mumbled apologies and from then on, watched over me.

I took the bus weekly to a physical therapist in lower Manhattan. I also saw a doctor who applied compresses with electrodes plugged in, that sent shock waves through my body. Not painful, just weird, tingling. I was encouraged to be active, to participate in sports: volleyball, softball, basketball, ping-pong, which I did all through school.

I have seen descriptions of children that ended up in iron lungs, and of the thousands that died from the disease. I was one of the lucky ones. What remains from that childhood ordeal is an orthotic that I am supposed to wear in my left shoe and usually forget, and a love of puzzles.

———————————

There are two kinds of people: Those that enjoy jigsaw puzzles and everyone else.

Aficionados of the hobby turn up their noses at most offerings; I have my own exacting standards. The imagery must be beautiful, or interesting. No banal, pretty artwork, aka Thomas Kincaid. Wit, drama, and color matter. More important than the image is the complexity of the cuts. The pieces must be varied; the worst is opening the box of your newly purchased 1,000-piece puzzle and discovering that each piece is an identical "little man," with a head, two arms and two legs. Deadly boring.

Certain brands are more to my liking. My personal favorites are *The New Yorker* magazine covers turned into puzzles, made by, appropriately, The New York Puzzle Company. Alas, my last puzzle from them was a charming image from a 1945 issue, but it was missing two pieces from the get-go, and instead, had two duplicates of existing pieces that didn't fit anywhere. Quality control, not at its best. But I consider that an anomaly and continue to buy their product as they apologized and offered me a substitute puzzle.

I see completing a complex jigsaw puzzle as a test of my mental status. Not sure it's one that a doctor would cite as a reliable cognition test, but to me, it says, "You're okay, your brain is still working."

# *Pushy Jew*

I once met a woman in town and when I introduced myself, she said, "Oh, I know who you are, you're the New Yorker."

What did she mean by that? There's nothing about my appearance that says New Yorker. It's not my accent. When people talk about "a New York accent," they mean "Brooklyn" or "the Bronx." I don't sound like that; I'm an upper West Side girl from Manhattan.

I think she was saying, you're the *Pushy New York Jew*. Her words implying a well-worn slur: loud, aggressive, moneygrubbing.

I didn't think much about being Jewish when I was growing up. At the private school I attended, almost all of my classmates were Jewish. At home, we celebrated the Jewish holidays. I dressed up as Queen

Esther for Purim. We fasted on Yom Kippur, the children making it to late afternoon when we were given a snack. We celebrated Hanukkah, not Christmas, with menorahs, presents, dreidels, and latkes.

My father belonged to a nearby synagogue. Dressed in my best clothes, I was the one who would go on the high holy days with him and his mother, the only grandparent I ever knew. She came weekly for dinner and read to me from the *Big Golden Book of Bible Stories* and held her monthly Hadassah meetings in our home.

After she died, I assumed I could stop attending religious services, but my father said, "Now you go for *me*." I didn't understand the Hebrew and found the services long and boring, but I never questioned why I was the only one who had to go; maybe I enjoyed being the special daughter on those occasions.

Of course, we celebrated the Passover Seder, the story of the Jews' exodus from Egypt. This springtime holiday brought all my father's New York relatives to our house — 20 people spread around a large, U-shaped table set with linen, flowers in tiny vases, the best china and cutlery. Everyone, even the children, had a wine glass and a Haggadah.

We dined on multiple courses of matzo ball soup, gefilte fish, brisket, kugel, salad, and Aunt Sidja's carrot cake. I ate everything except the carp, an enormous beast that my mother had delivered live from a fish market on Columbus Avenue, and which appeared in two guises: ground up and shaped into large mounds that were poached, or whole pieces, including the head, cooked in a yellowish jelly. The eyes stared up at me as the platter was passed around.

My father sat at the head of the table, I sat on his right. The other children, my sisters and cousins, sat at the other end where there was much laughter and clowning around.

My father was a showman. He read the story with great drama in both English and Hebrew. Growing up in Vienna, he'd learned multiple languages. When he came across a passage he particularly liked, he'd read it again, sometimes in German, maybe in French.

I found the evenings interminable, and I envied the other kids. Today, other family members host the Seder, and I find myself again seated at the head of the table, as I have become the family matriarch, the oldest of the American-born clan still alive.

I love the Seder now. I imagine Jews around the world saying the same words and singing the same songs and I think, *We are still here.*

As a child, I had blonde curls and looked like Shirley Temple. My looks still don't identify me as Jewish (and what exactly does a Jew look like?). Perhaps that's why people have frequently used the expression "Jew you down" in my presence.

When my husband and I were newlyweds living in a small town outside Chicago, anti-Semitic comments were so common that I tried to head them off by introducing myself, "Hi, I'm Judy, I'm Jewish." My best friend, a tall, blonde Norwegian Protestant, cringed when I did that and convinced me to stop.

From the age of five, my sisters and I attended a Jewish girls camp in Maine, where I learned to horse-back ride. One summer as a teen, I begged to go to a different camp in Vermont, to learn how to jump. I was assigned Jack, a mean, ugly gelding.

There was a particular saddle that helped me stay on as Jack leapt with confidence over the fences. I asked if I could use it regularly. That evening, the camp owners called me into their office. Yes, I could use the saddle. But they lectured me on the dangers of being seen as "pushy." They said they were doing me a favor, "Because you're Jewish, you have to be careful, not to be so aggressive," one said, "People will judge you unkindly."

Mortified, I didn't say anything to my parents until the summer was over. My father wrote them a scathing letter and I never went back.

When I applied to colleges, an advisor from Northwestern University told me I met all their qual-ifications, but that, "Our Jewish quota is filled for the year." (Today, I doubt anyone would say such a thing to one's face, but the quota might still exist, just unspoken.)

Then there was the blind date with a young man arranged by one of my mother's friends. His family was upset that he was seeing an "older Gentile woman," and they were desperate to fix him up with a Jewish girl.

I remember just two things from that evening. While waiting in line at a movie theater to buy tickets, as I was chattering away, he interrupted me to say, "Don't talk with your hands, it's so Jewish." Later in our seats, during the black-and-white newsreel of important world events that ran prior to the feature film, Pope Pius XII, who had recently died, was shown in profile, laid out in his glass coffin. My date turned to me and said, "You have a nose just like his!"

There was no second date.

But the expression, "it's so Jewish," said with dripping contempt, became a catchphrase and source of great amusement between my sisters and me.

It wasn't until college that I lived among non-Jews and realized that there was a wider world where not everyone was Jewish. My roommate went to church on Sundays. Our holidays were different. When David, my future husband, and I bought our first home in a New Jersey suburb, a neighborhood child, maybe 10 or 11, came over and was exploring the piles of trash left in the garage with my eldest son when they discovered a small crucifix. My son didn't know what it was, but the girl held it up and explained to him, "this is dead God."

These incidents usually made me mortified or embarrassed. But when a neighbor once said to me, "I should have been Jewish; I just love bagels," what I experienced was rage. I remember thinking, *You ignorant bitch, if I could make you Jewish with a wave of my hand, I would. Spend nine hours watching the documentary "Shoah" and then tell me you wish you were Jewish.*

Being Jewish isn't about liking bagels. It's about living with contradictions. About being an outsider and "the Chosen People." It's about being a citizen of a country but also a part of "Ahm Y'israel" — the people of Israel. About sharing a 2,000-year-old history and living in the modern world.

When I lived in Israel, I marveled at the fact that, as almost everyone was Jewish, nobody called you, "Dirty Kike." Instead, they insulted one another with a rich string of expletives, usually in Arabic, that included obscenities about your mother, the size of your brain or your sexual organs, but never the word "Jew."

Today, I live in "East Bumfuck," as my husband used to call this small New England town, southeast of Hartford. I live mostly among *goyim*, non-Jews, but it is only around Easter or Christmas, when my home decorations are of six-pointed Jewish stars, that I am the odd duck, the stranger in a strange land. Most of the time, I am just the old lady who lives in the cool house on the corner and paints stuff.

Before we moved here, I made note that it had a small synagogue. That was important to me, whether I joined the congregation or not. I didn't want to live somewhere and be the only Jew in town.

Several years ago, as I had once taken a "cloud" painting class, I volunteered to paint those billowing shapes on the building's ceiling. It was a foolish offer, as I am afraid of heights. My husband did what he could. He bolted his ladder to scaffolding, modified it with railings and floorboards, but to no avail. High in the air, as I worked my way around the ceiling, my feet clung to the planks like a limpet. Terror and fatigue finally outweighed my dedication, and the finished mural is of a gradually clearing sky, the clouds growing fewer and farther apart.

I don't attend that synagogue anymore. Still, this pushy Jew has certainly left her mark.

# Make 'em Laugh

$A$ friend recently commented that my personal stories are funny and glib, but I don't "dig deep enough."

It's true, I will make a joke out of everything.

I think it's a Jewish thing, born from the instinct that if they're laughing at you (Nazis, Klansmen, religious fundamentalists), they're less likely to kill you.

Tell me I'm wrong.

It's not that I don't take things seriously, it's just the way I deal with adversity. But I joke even in non-life-threatening situations. Does that mean I'm a frivolous person? Or avoid hard issues? I don't think so. On things that matter to me (family, our planet, justice), I take Rabbi Hillel's dictum to heart, "What you yourself hate, don't do to your neighbor," and try to live my life that way. But I also see absurdity around me every day, and if not laughing, I'd probably cry.

My mother didn't have much of a sense of humor, but my father did. He told me my first joke when I was about 10. A silly, visual one, involving a princess who shows a shit-soiled finger to her father and demands that it be cut off; the king suggests she just wash her hand, but she insists. He finally agrees and calls in his executioner. The princess puts her finger on the chopping block, the executioner raises his axe, and as he brings it down, she jerks her finger back and pops it in her mouth.

You gotta see it in person.

Maybe it sticks in my mind because it was a "dirty" joke — the word he used was "Kaka," Yiddish for shit, a word I wasn't allowed to say; maybe because my father told it to me, I felt special.

Today, my taste in humor is a little different, here's my personal favorite:

*A man is hiking in the Alps, and while walking on a narrow trail as dusk is approaching, he slips and falls. As he tumbles off the side of the mountain, he manages to grab a small branch sticking out from a crevice. It stops his fall and clinging to it he calls out, "Help me, help me!" A voice responds from the gloom, "Let go of the branch, my son, and I will lift you up." The man hesitates ... "Is there anybody else?"*

If you don't think that's both funny and profound, we probably won't be friends.

As to whether I should write more deeply. Not gonna happen. I don't intend to spell out my emotions more fully on the page. I think you, dear reader, can do some work, draw your own conclusions.

# All Grown Up

# The Pasha

Before I was married to David, my childhood sweetheart, I was married, briefly, to an Israeli. I don't recommend that; in my limited experience, Israelis are like a fine wine, best enjoyed in their home country. "The Pasha" was what my mother called my first husband. Here's how he came — and went — from my life.

After my ignominious experience at Syracuse University, my parents packed me off to Israel where several of my mother's sisters lived, having emigrated there before World War II. I had visited Israel briefly when I graduated from high school. This time I went in disgrace. But I found living on the kibbutz in Northern Galilee a wonderful, restorative experience (see *Jack of all Trades*).

After almost a year in the kibbutz, I moved to a small, one-room flat in Hadera, a seaside town midway between Tel Aviv and Haifa. There I studied Hebrew at an *ulpan*, an intensive language learning course, with the idea that I would get a job and stay in Israel.

The *ulpan* was a mixed bag of people from all over. I became good friends with several. There was David from England, a Dutch girl whose name I forget, and Movita, a sophisticated divorcee from France who advised me on skin care (telling me that as I aged I would have to decide "between my face and my figure, I couldn't have both.")

That's where I met my first husband.

He had just completed his two-year compulsory military service. He was handsome, albeit with terrible teeth. (My mother had always said, before you marry, look at his teeth and his wallet. If he has bad teeth, it will cost you thousands in dental work for your children.) I ignored her advice and managed to marry two men, both with bad teeth. She was right.

His best friend and he were thinking about what to do next. They eventually decided to take up an offer to go to Germany where they would be trained as managers for a company that was opening a manufacturing plant in Israel.

That should have been the end of our relationship, but he suggested marriage and that I accompany him to Germany. I had nothing else happening in my life, no direction, no plans, so I said "yes" and wrote my parents. Big mistake.

My father responded that if he wanted to learn a trade, he could come to America and learn the shoe business. From that moment, I was swept up in a tsunami of activity that overtook me and swept me along. My family came to Israel, the small wedding we'd planned in a local wedding hall became a huge affair at a Hilton. Then on to Germany, where my father had connections in the shoe business, and my new hubby could train and learn the shoe business before we moved to the United States.

I thought I was pleasing my parents: I was not just marrying a Jew (none of my previous boyfriends had been Jewish), but an Israeli! My father was enthusiastic, my mother took one look, and disliked him from the start. She thought he was a chauvinist, a bully, and untrustworthy. She said he behaved like a *pasha* — expecting to be waited on.

When he didn't want to do something, he would shrug and say, "*Ahnee Lo Yachol.*" ("I cannot.") She said I allowed it; I did. He was in a strange land, new job, newlywed, he knew no one besides me. Give him a break, I thought.

The night before the wedding, I wrote to David to tell him.

Germany was awful. We stayed in a pleasant enough inn, and he went each morning to the factory. I sat and did nothing. Finally, I went to see the company president, and begged him to give me a job — anything, he didn't have to pay me, just something to keep me occupied.

That's how I ended up in the shoe company's shipping department, where I had one of the most humiliating experiences of my life, and also learned some valuable lessons.

My task was to pack boxes with the heels of women's shoes. The heels were in bins labeled with their sizes, 6, 7, 8, and so on. He said to put the heels in a plastic bag and drop it in a carton. "*Zehn*," he said. I knew enough German: "Ten."

He left, and I went to work. I was conscientious and fast. Workers remarked about the American girl and how swift I was — twice the speed of the German employees! After two days, the foreman came back to check on me. Watching me, he stopped me, shaking his head, "*zehn paar!*" Ten pairs.

I was twice as fast because I was packing half as many. I was packing ten heels, not ten pairs of heels.

Production stopped. All the boxes I had packed had to be retrieved, opened, sorted, and repacked.

We worked for … was it only one day? Two? I don't remember. I do remember that no one spoke to this American wunderkind the entire time.

That was the end of my work experience in Germany. He finished his training, and we went to England, another factory, more training — and I was alone all day. What did I do with my time? It is a total blank. My memory is of him spending evenings spying on a couple who lived in an apartment building across from us who left their shades open. When we left to come to the States, I was pregnant with my first child.

The only other memory is of a fight that we had outside our building, about what I haven't a clue, and that I was so angry that I spit at him (the first and last time I've ever done such a thing). He wiped his face and we walked into our building and when we got in the elevator, he slapped me hard in the face.

No one had ever hit me before and I was stunned. I probably deserved the slap, but the fact that he waited until we were alone in the elevator never left me. He knew it was wrong, he made sure no one saw.

That was the beginning of the end of the marriage.

I remember telling this story to David, also that I cried a lot in that marriage. From frustration, rage, self-pity. David found that hard to believe, as he had never seen me cry.

The slap became a topic of great amusement between my sisters and me when I went through my divorce. My attorney taking their deposition explained he would ask several questions: one was "Did you ever see him hit her?" My sisters practiced various responses: "*I* never saw him strike her," I never *saw* him strike her," "I never saw him strike *her* ... " all variations with damning implications.

In the USA, in our small townhouse apartment in Harrisburg, we both tried. But when I found out that he was having sex with women in the factory, and at our apartment, in my bed, when I was visiting my parents in New York City with the baby, that was it. I left him, took my son, and moved back home and filed for divorce.

I never saw him again.

Looking back at this period of my life, I am astonished at how pliable and undirected I was. I was in my early 20s but immature, bending to other's whims and desires; trying to please them. That is not the woman I am today.

# My One and Only

It's Valentine's Day and couples are celebrating. I have nothing to celebrate. Instead, I remember.

One person really loved me, and he's gone, 15 years this June.

Married for more than 40 years, we knew each other for 54, ever since he showed up, a new kid in class, 12 years old, black hair, a blue shirt with yellow lightning-bolt inserts on the shoulders that his grandmother made for him. He sat in the back of the room, with the other troublemakers; I in the front row — the good girl, always prepared, ready to answer.

He was my childhood sweetheart.

We lived 10 blocks apart. I, in a 10-room high-rise with five bathrooms and doormen, he and his family in a five-room apartment with one bathroom and a buzzer to get in. On his first visit he marveled that "everyone could go to the bathroom at the same time." His stepfather was a communist, a typesetter at a Hungarian newspaper. My father owned shoe factories in eastern Pennsylvania.

I called him up after my divorce and return to the city. He took me to Central Park to watch a lunar eclipse. We started dating. He invited me to his family's Christmas party and told his mother he was bringing someone (she remembered me from high school), and that he was going to marry me. We were married the following June.

He was as handsome a man as he was a boy, with the same 32-inch waist all his life. He had little vanity, but when it became clear that he was going bald, he shaved his head, keeping a handlebar mustache that he groomed and curled. He lived in jeans and cowboy boots with pointy toes. "Don't your feet hurt"? I asked after a long day in high heels. "Never," he replied. The boots remain on the top shelf of the closet.

It was always me.

He thought I was smart, beautiful, and capable; I could do anything. He supported my every job, each creative endeavor. He made his living as an industrial designer, creating prototypes for products to be manufactured. A client said he had "golden hands"; he was the one who could do anything.

He bought clever and wonderful gifts, but best were the things he did to make my life better, easier, my surroundings more beautiful. Turning the basement into an artist's studio, borrowing a backhoe to make a 30-foot pond in the backyard with a meandering stream and waterfall. He moved walls, built coffee tables, shelving, and installed lighting throughout our home. And because it mattered to me, he learned to dance at age 50. His favorites were swing and the waltz. Photos capture us: me smiling up at him, as he frowns in concentration while he twirls me round.

Funny — and fun — he bought his sons gifts on Father's Day as thanks for making him a Dad. He cut their sandwiches into their initials, taught them how to ride bikes and play ball, made kites and rockets with them, built the best-ever treehouse that neighborhood kids, now grown, still recall. Willing to look silly, at Halloween he dressed as King Kong to my Fay Wray, or Death with black hood and scythe when I went as Taxes.

Car rides together we debated and argued: should Pete Rose be accepted into the Baseball Hall of Fame? Why not Jesse Jackson for President? Michelangelo or Picasso, which was the more influential artist? When we reached our destination, he would let me take his hand, although public displays of affection embarrassed him.

Because he was soft-spoken, rarely raising his voice, and I was loud and pushy, people assumed I ruled the roost, called the shots.

So not true!

It was more he was a lone bull walking in a pasture, and I was the herding dog running in circles around him, jumping and barking, while he just kept going steadily in the direction he wanted.

He worked alone. Friends came through shared activities, like bicycling. He went yearly to RAGBRAI, that weeklong bike ride across Iowa. He asked me to join him, I declined; he didn't need me there, he was happy with his fellow peddlers. Among his many bicycles was a tandem, and we did ride together once, with me on the back seat as "stoker." I announced we could stay married or ride together; not both.

After 9/11, he needed "to do something useful" and studied to become a paramedic with an ambulance company. On his first day at work, someone stole his jacket, newly purchased with the paramedic's patch I'd sewn on the sleeve the night before. He reported the theft and said if it wasn't returned, he was resigning, as he wouldn't work for a company where employees stole from each other. The jacket reappeared the next day.

He got sicker, weaker, his blood transfusions increasing to twice a week. His veins were collapsing but he refused to let them insert a port, which would have made the whole procedure easier. "Easier for you," he told them, "Not for me." The prognosis was grim, he got thinner, his clothes hanging off him. He kept working.

The void he left is a bottomless pit. Friends, projects, chores — they fill the days, but don't touch the tender core of his absence. I rattle around in this too-big house, I should move to something smaller. But how can I? He is present in every room.

I get older, he is fixed in time, in the finite number of photos of him that exist. I know them all by heart.

# Love and Marriage

I am attracted to opposites. Lovers, spouses, friends, they are usually nothing like me. Once in therapy, I stated I wanted to be "the center of my husband's world." That was one of the dumber things I've said and knew it as soon as the words were out of my mouth.

All those platitudes, "He's my better half, "He completes me," our relationship was nothing like that. He thought I was smart and beautiful, I thought he was the handsomest, cleverest man in the room who could make and fix anything. We stayed together for 41 years because it worked for each of us.

He asked me on our 30th anniversary if we could go another 30? I said, half-seriously — "We'll see … something better might come along."

Did I deserve him? No. Did I appreciate him? Absolutely. Was it idyllic? Absolutely not. We were so different, in our tastes, our experiences, our ways of dealing with conflict. And yet ... others would look at us and think we had a terrific marriage, maybe because we liked each other and were happy in each other's company. That affection continued long after the honeymoon phase.

It didn't start out well. When we had a disagreement, he would simply withdraw. He never fought. He hated confrontation and tried to avoid it by leaving, while to me his refusal to stay and have it out was my mother's withholding all over again. I couldn't bear it; it infuriated me.

I would throw things at him, screaming, "Don't you walk away from me!" I would start a fight with him in public, in private — made no difference. To me, he was David, but when I was angry, he became Dave. That's what the guys in the fire department called him, and I'd say, "Oh really, Dave?" Is that what you think, Dave?" I was a real bitch.

We got better at it: he learned to stay put; I learned to stop yelling. We always made up.

In our first year of marriage, he bought me a housecoat as a birthday present. It was hideous. Mid-calf in length, a Peter Pan collar, ecru lace over pale blue satin, it would have been appropriate for his grandmother. I was stunned. Is that how he saw me? I tried it on and struggled with not wanting to hurt his feelings and being honest. I gave up and told him. He listened, packed it up and came back a few days later with a different, beautiful robe: a flowing caftan of diaphanous saffron chiffon that still hangs in my closet.

I love to cook, yet I learned he ate almost nothing. Early in the marriage, I made a pork-chop-coated-in-mustard recipe. "What the fuck is that smell!" he said as he walked in the door. I cried, threw out the dinner. I discovered his only condiment was ketchup. Mustard, vinegar, mayonnaise, salad dressing, hollandaise sauce, all off the menu.

The lunches I packed him each day were pathetic. I complained that others seeing the sparse fixings would think he had a neglectful wife: two pieces of rye bread, a slice of American cheese and maybe, maybe, a slice of boiled ham, Pepsi (never Coke), Oreo cookies and maybe an orange. He loved sweets, and fortunately — fruit.

He grew up in a single-mom household close to his grandparents, who lived in the Bronx. His grandmother, Bubi, a small, soft-spoken woman who spoke little English and was a superb seamstress, was a miserable cook (as was his mother, although she made a very good flan). In defense, he and his grandfather,

Zedi, ate little, preferring plain dishes, whenever they could. Eventually I discovered favorites that he liked: a lasagna that was heavy on the sausage and ground beef, broiled lamb chops, breaded chicken cutlets, cheeseburgers. He joked that his favorite vegetable was mint jelly.

When he died, I couldn't decide what to do with his ashes. I thought about scattering them at a place he loved but knew the instant they were in the air I would regret it. Several years before we had visited a high school friend in California and gone walking in Muir Woods. He loved the stillness and majesty of the place. He told me then he'd like his ashes scattered there. I laughed and said if I'd known, I would have paid for a lifetime pass, not the day tickets we'd just purchased. But in reality, I could not leave them in a place so far away from me.

I thought about burying them in front of his workshop, but if I moved from this house that was our last home together, I would have to dig them up and take them with me. I couldn't bear to leave him behind. A friend rolled his eyes at that idea and persuaded me to find another, more permanent solution, so I created a sarcophagus. It's a box decorated with paint, gel films of photos on its interior, and topped with symbols of David's passions. He would have found it charming and clever.

It is not for public gazing; it waits on top of the dresser in my bedroom.

I did take a small vial of the remains with me to California and left them as promised, in Muir Woods. I have a photo of the spot.

I have told my youngest son that when I die, I wish to be cremated, and our ashes mixed and buried (or scattered — where is immaterial, as long as we are together; I thought maybe in Central Park, where we used to make out when we were young). I showed him the painted box, he thought it was cool — but I shall leave a note inside repeating my instructions, maybe include suggestions on mixing the two sets of ashes.

That's me, micromanaging to the end.

# Why a Pond?

Fish and I go way back, which is ironic, as I dislike eating them. But they were an integral part of my childhood relationship with my father: our first bond was fishing together on summer weekends in Long Island Sound, on his boat, the Siboney, named for the transport ship that brought him to America.

The other bond was raising tropical fish together in our apartment. The creation of a tiny aquatic ecosystem was an ongoing commitment. Lights and heaters have to be turned on and off, filters changed, pumps repaired, fish fed daily. But it never ceased to intrigue and delight me.

I don't remember if David's family had an aquarium when he was a boy. Probably not, as their apartment was small, but he happily got into it. When we were first married and living in an apartment where no pets were allowed, it seemed only natural to add a fish tank. Tropical fish doesn't actually count as "pets" (you can't scratch behind their ears, they don't lie on your lap, and they don't bark or purr). But there's a reason doctors' offices have aquariums in their waiting rooms (albeit rather boring ones, with few fish and not much variety). They're fun to watch.

Our ambitions expanded beyond tanks of fish when we bought our first home in New Jersey, and a landscape architect designed a pond for us next to our home. It was a two-level affair on a slope between the house and the driveway. The upper pond was about 30 feet across and had a waterfall into the lower pond, which was slightly smaller.

There was a three-foot-wide wooden plank bridge less than a foot above the water that ran between the two sides. I would lie on my stomach peering between the slats at the fish that huddled under the bridge in the heat of the day. One day as my eyes adjusted to the light as I stared down, I was shocked to see an enormous snake coiled up directly below me. Heart pounding, I scrambled up and away as slowly as I could control.

To stock the pond, David had brought home small, cheap goldfish that cost pennies. I don't remember plants, but it did have floating duckweed, which spreads across the surface and provides shade and protection for the fish from aerial predators. I wonder if the people who bought our house kept it. I've never been back to check if it's still there.

When we moved to Connecticut, David decided he would build a new pond by himself.

It wasn't easy — or cheap. Between the stones that always needs resetting, the pump that frequently jams, the filters that need changing, the net that takes at least two people to install in the fall to catch the falling leaves and then remove in the spring, having it emptied, drained, scrubbed and refilled every spring, is costly. Sometimes I think about draining it, filling it in with soil. But it was a labor of love, one of the many gifts David created and so here it stays.

Here how he did it:

- Borrow a backhoe to dig the hole. *David's a city boy, how does he know how to do this?*
- Remove boulders. *There's a reason so many towns around here are named Rocky Hill, Rocky Neck, East Rock, Rock Ridge.*
- Carve out a stream that starts at the corner of the house and meanders downhill to spill over a waterfall into the pond. *I direct, David digs.*
- Line the hole with newspaper. *A neighbor with a flooring store provides carpet scraps and remnants.*
- Create two raised, flat areas along the perimeter. *These will be for marsh plants.*

- Order a custom-made rubberized liner online. *The most expensive part of this endeavor.*
- Wait for it to arrive. *It takes several weeks.*
- Install the liner in the hole and stream bed.
- Edge everything with small rocks.
- Buy gravel. *A truck delivers a small mountain of it into our driveway. One wheelbarrow at a time, we haul it to the backyard to line the stream and plant beds.*
- Add a sump pump and piping to circulate and re-cycle the water.
- Border the exterior edge with large flat stones.
- Slowly fill the pond with a hose. *After three days, the well is running dry, and the pond is not even half full.*
- Wait one week, do again. *Slowly, this time.*
- Add aquatic plants, those that like "wet feet." *Cattails, reeds, flag iris, water lettuce, and pickerel reed with its plumes of lavender flowers.*
- Add fish. *Buy five small koi, they disappear overnight. A Heron? Raccoons? Who knows?*
- For the price of one koi, David buys a dozen small goldfish at a local pet store. These are "feeder fish"; people buy them to feed to their piranhas and reptiles. *Over the years, they die off, and we buy more, selecting each fish carefully, looking for healthy specimens with long tail fins. Most will survive over the years, multiply and grow huge. Some do not; a giant blue heron visits the pond, and there are raccoons.*

- Feed them from spring through autumn, every few days. *When the first pellets hit the surface, they converge on the surface and devour everything. Neighborhood children like to help; I ration out portions, or they would throw in too much, fouling the water.*
- Purchase more fish. Some survive, others are wiped out by a sudden spring freeze, or a rapacious raccoon who won't take no for an answer.
- As I write this there is a school of 35 bright orange goldfish, a few white ones with red blotches, several blacks, and two metallic yellow koi.
- There are jellied sacs of peeper eggs among the reeds. These small frogs croak on spring and summer evenings. Sometimes a large black snake swims among the fish, salamanders abound. Occasionally there are small garter snakes. In spring there are dragonflies, and swarms of tiny bugs that skate across the pond's surface. At dusk, the bats swoop low over the water, catching insects. The murmur of the running water can be heard through open windows.

Maybe the appeal of this backyard watery world is the same that attracts visitors to public aquariums or zoos. To experience nature, and different ecosystems. With a fish tank or a pond, maybe it's the chance to play God.

It's simple, really: dig a hole, fill with water, life happens.

# Daniel

I don't want to write about him. It will revive all the fights, the drama, the police, therapists, the hours of counseling, the reality of my failures to be the mother I wanted to be and instead, reveal the mother I was.

I love him, I hate him, I fear him, I've wished he were dead.

"Now, I must deal with him alone," I thought when my husband died; just another level of anguish and despair piled onto my already overwhelming grief.

He was the most beautiful child I've ever seen. All mothers think that, I suppose, but he really was extraordinary. There's a photo, he's maybe two years old, sitting up, naked on a towel on the grass, smiling. He resembled the cherubs you see painted on church rotundas — all plump golden body and curls, only missing their wings. He was adorable and adored. Quick to learn, he loved science, reading, acting in school plays. In his teens he took up technical rock climbing and practicing by scaling the large mulberry tree in our backyard with just his hands and feet. He went climbing (with whom? I don't remember), in the Shawangunk Mountain ridge in New York. Agile, nimble, he was a bright, happy, and inquisitive boy.

He is no longer beautiful. In the infrequent pictures he sends, he is scary looking. Overweight, long, tangled hair down to his shoulders, with few remaining teeth, he has been in and out of prisons and mental hospitals for most of his adult life. He rents a room in a house on the other side of the country. Diagnosed as mentally ill, he lives on government disability and hounds me for money. Articulate, with an incredible vocabulary, he is brilliantly funny, loving, and vicious.

We communicate via email, as I have blocked him from my home phone, which I changed to an unlisted number after too many late night phone calls, 10 to 20 in a row.

What kind of mother does that?

When did it all fall apart? In high school when he started using drugs? Or when he dropped out of school? We gave him choices: "Go back to school, get a job, or leave." He did all three. He got a job, passed his GED, and left to follow the Grateful Dead.

Was it the accident on a Kentucky highway when the VW bus he was driving was rear-ended by a semi and he went through the windshield into a guard-rail? He survived, but suffered a fractured skull, a major concussion, and a shattered left leg. The phone call in the middle of the night, the flight to the hospital emergency room, his face battered and swollen, unrecognizable. He recovered and left against medical advice, with friends, heading to California where he successfully sued the trucker who hit him. He lived off that money for the next 40 years, until it was all gone.

Was it my fault? Was I such a bad mother? He had a stepfather who loved him and yet, he went in search of his birth father, only to be rejected when he found him. Would a different outcome have made a difference? Would anything?

What's the point of reliving it all?

There was a time, years ago, when he was in one of his "normal" periods, (bipolar being part of his diag-nosis, schizophrenia being the other), he attended a community college. I encouraged it, and he did well, he enjoyed the classes, and then ... it fell apart. Even-tually, they asked him to withdraw. His decline was devastating. I wanted him to be normal. I wanted my golden boy back.

Instead, his life became a cycle of arrests, hospital-izations, and recovery. Rinse and repeat.

Recently, he had written that he intended to come East and visit the special school in Vermont that he'd attended as a teenager. I advised against it (that school no longer exists), and I never heard about it again.

And then, on the second day of summer, he emailed to say that he'd been picked up for hitchhiking in my state, sentenced to 90 days incarceration, and had just been released. He was using a computer in a public library on the other end of the state. Could I help him retrieve his belongings, a backpack, his leather jacket?

The next 48 hours were a lesson in bureaucratic incompetence, cruelty, and carelessness.

I enlist a friend, a retired male nurse used to working with psychiatric patients, to come with me, and we drive the 80 miles to the public library. I recognize my son — but barely. Long, tangled graying hair, practically toothless, a twisted left leg that sticks out at an angle. The grey eyes are the same. He's wearing a mishmash of ill-fitting clothing the prison provided. We drive back to the correctional facility to get his belongings.

The man who assured me on the phone that his belongs will be at the "front desk" is wrong. There is no front desk, no one to speak with, just a white bulletproof glass wall, where a disembodied voice emanates from a small slit, stating that, "You need to make an appointment." There is no one to complain to, to demand answers from. A police officer appears, shrugs, there is no sign of his backpack, jacket. He says my son has 30 days to write requesting his belongings, they will be sent to his address, and then he hands over four slips of paper — each is good for one day's bus travel within the state.

My son is homeless. He has no "address" to send his belongings to. Sayonara.

He is not angry, or even surprised. It is not his first rodeo. He does, however, opine that he thought the justice system "is supposed to be punitive, not inhumane." I am livid with rage.

We head home and stop at a diner where I buy the three of us a late lunch. My son and my friend the nurse chat about music, he eats little. We drop my friend back at his home and hit a local Goodwill (a store he knows well, one I usually donate items to). He picks out a backpack, three T-shirts, a pair of pants, then on to a T-Mobile store to buy him a new cellphone, then to a motel near the airport, his choice — I had weakened and said he could stay with me, but he prefers a motel, "if you won't be offended." I am relieved.

Once home, I sit at my computer and book him a flight back to Seattle for the next day. From the nearest airport, it's not a straight shot, he must change planes and it's expensive. I get him window seats.

Next morning I pick him up. We breakfast at McDonald's, he prefers to eat in the car. He is wearing his new clothes; we hit L.L. Bean for a windbreaker and a discount shoe store for black sneakers — I joke he will be the best dressed homeless person when he returns to the West Coast. We sit in my living room and he looks at my photo albums. He asks to take three of the photos, saves others on his new phone. We head to the airport. We hug, he thanks me profusely, and he is gone.

Will I ever see him again? Elton John's "Daniel," plays in my head; I grit my teeth, take deep breaths, determined not to cry.

# *Baby Bird*

He looked like a baby bird when he was born, a head of spiky dark hair, big blue eyes. His birth almost killed me.

A complication occurred during the delivery and I developed a high fever that only got worse. Instead of going home, I was moved to the ICU for several terrifying days where I was laid on a rubber sheet covered with a bed of ice in an attempt to get my fever down. I joked that I felt like a shrimp cocktail, but it wasn't funny at all. David was terrified, I was upset that I was on so many drugs, and I wasn't allowed to nurse my baby.

I survived, as did my son, but it decided us: no more children. We would be happy with our two boys.

A happy child, he loved science, cats, and tiny

things — a button, an acorn, a seashell, objects that he kept in a clear plastic box with small compartments. He had a favorite blanket — his "blankie," that he took wherever we went.

A cheerful, curious boy. He's a lefty, like his mother, and loved to draw detailed images of spaceships and astronauts. And then there was skating. The town had built an ice rink just a few blocks from our home and when we first took him there, he fell frequently. But instead of crying or complaining, he immediately got up and tried again, and again; he just kept going.

By the time he was seven, the skates were like part of his body and as he grew, he became a "rink rat," spending all his time there after school, sharpening skates and helping out. While he played other sports, skating was and is his passion. When he started playing hockey, the bag to hold all his gear was bigger than he was, and his father would carry it until he grew taller and stronger. Today, he co-captains a team in an adult league, still usually the smallest player. Watching him on the ice, I feel *nachas*, joy.

When he was nine, he suffered a horrific accident. Our family was attending a friend's summer pool party, and my son and a friend had gone inside. Now he came running down the stairs, straight into the sliding glass door, which usually was open, but not this time. The sound of the shattering glass (not tempered, not safety), brought us all to attention.

Everything then happened in slow motion, vignettes of images. Him standing inside the house, stunned, his hands covering his face, me leaping from my chair poolside, running, cutting my hand on the shards of glass in the doorframe, unable to pull it open, stepping through the opening, scooping him up in my arms. The wound on his leg a gaping chasm: sinew, bone, muscles, blood. Others come and help wrap a towel around it. Someone calls for an ambulance.

We wait. I thought he would die in my arms.

His father and I ride with him in the ambulance. At the hospital while someone stitches my hand, an orthopedic surgeon repairs his left leg; he had severed a tendon. He is sewn up, put in a cast and given a boot to protect his foot (I later painted it to look like a rabbit). The five-inch scar across his shin remains.

He became a Boy Scout — his father helped him with earning badges, not me. He went to scout camp in New Mexico, reluctantly, but ended up loving it. Inside, he is still a boy scout. He is always ready to lend a hand to a neighbor, he will stop to help at an accident scene. He is unflappable, hardworking and kind, one of the good guys.

He always had beautiful, smart girlfriends, up to and including the girl he finally married. He met her at the electrical company he worked for before he went out on his own. Others warned her away from him, "Watch out for the silver-tongued Jew," they said. He was unfazed by the casual anti-Semitism and won her affections with his easy smile and humor. He studied and passed the exam to become a master electrician. The "gentlemen's trade," as he calls it — so much better than being a plumber.

In middle age, he loves being a dad. That he has daughters delights him. He yells at them — too often. But they seem to know the difference between "just noise" and "serious," and adore him.

His father was his hero. He wants to be like him, and they are alike in so many ways. He is much more social — his dad was a loner, preferring solitary bike rides. The son is a people person, a team player. He has the best of both of us: his father's skills and the gene to help others. My sense of humor and way with words.

A grown man when his father died, he still misses him. They used to go together to RAGBRAI, the week-long bike ride across Iowa that they did every summer. He would party nightly until dawn, sleep briefly and somehow complete the ride no worse for wear.

He started attending community college in his 20s, and then stopped. I don't remember why. His wife is encouraging him to go back and finish. He resists — fear of failing? Or because he loves surprising customers that the blue-collar electrician they're talking to is articulate, intelligent, and knowledge-able? We'll see. My money's on her.

Midlife, he is still my baby boy. I will not be around to see how his life turns out, but I am pretty sure it will have a happy ending. He is a work in progress.

# Open Wide

**W**hy write about my teeth? All I can say is that I once contemplated writing a book, "Dentists I Have Known and Left." While of long standing, the dental profession and I have not had a mutually rewarding relationship.

The issue started when as a child, I had no cavities. Our family dentist was tall, saturnine, and never smiled. The only thing I ever remember him saying was, "Spit, there," pointing to the bowl. I assumed he didn't like me, and perhaps he didn't, as there were no wisdom teeth, braces, fillings, or any real dental problems for him to solve. All he ever had to do was clean my teeth.

Today, he wouldn't even do that, he would have a hygienist do it. I had a gum abscess in my early

30s, which, as I already had one child, I can say with confidence, was as painful, if not worse, than child-birth. If I could have removed my head, I would have.

The real problems began after I got my first cavities when I was pregnant, a not uncommon occurrence, I learned. After that, it was downhill all the way. The first dentist who saw the writing on the wall said, "you have beautiful teeth; they will fall out of your mouth."

The issue was my gums. I had periodontal disease. I expect that's where the expression "long in the tooth" must come from, as the solution, surgery (multiple times, awful), requires lowering the gum away from the base of the tooth, making one look older and well ... long in the tooth.

My husband rarely went to the dentist. I don't think they had the money when he was a child. But other than brushing, which he did in a perfunctory manner, he didn't take care of his teeth, and as he aged they got worse and worse until eventually he needed dentures.

At that point his physical health had deteriorated considerably, but he finally said yes. The cost was horrific, thousands of dollars, as we had no dental insurance. Briefly I contemplated the reality that it was a waste of money; he was dying. But I agreed and he went for the fittings. When he finally got them, it made him feel better about himself, so it was worth it, even for the short time that remained.

It hasn't been all bad. There was a lovely dentist, Dr. T., in New Jersey who started the long, painful road of keeping my teeth in my mouth. He taught dentistry at a local college, and while he was working on my mouth, rather than listen to the sound of the instruments cutting and whacking away inside my mouth, I asked him to talk to me. So, he gave me "Dentistry 101."

That was good for about four visits, and then he just stopped talking. When I asked why (on the rare breaks when I was allowed to spit, drink water, or take a breath), he shrugged and said, "the rest is all slides." I retaliated by croaking out, "Flee! Flee!" to his waiting room full of patients as I stumbled away with an ice pack covering my mouth.

Another dentist, a specialist, was responsible for inserting a sort of armature inside my mouth to hold onto my teeth. He had the most beautiful office of any medical professional I've ever been to. The interior was not created from some dental furnishings catalog; these were personal choices. There was beautiful artwork hanging on the walls, a great color palette, and interesting mobiles hanging overhead (which really matters at a dentist since that's what you're looking at most of the time).

He himself was quite a dandy. He dressed in pinstripe suits, and I recall once noting that his footwear included black-and-white spats. The whole experience was delightful and every dental visit after that has been dull in comparison.

Another dentist, Dr. G., continued the lifelong process of holding onto my teeth. It meant more procedures, more pain, and more money. But he also whitened my teeth; I had no idea such a thing was possible, but it was, and he did, and it brightened my smile, and my life.

Today I never actually see a dentist on a regular basis, but go quarterly to a hygienist, a lovely Asian-American woman who fills the time while scraping away like a rat at my molars with tales about her children and her home life.

At this point, I can say with 98 percent certainty, that these teeth are here for the duration. Knock on wood.

# The Hardest Thing...

**...is** watching someone you love die. My father at 59, my mother 27 years later. Both of my older sisters, my childhood best friend, work colleagues, members of my women's group, drinking buddies. Some went quickly, some took weeks, months or even years. The hardest was the death of David, my husband.

It's difficult to remember now when his illness began. He started leaving his tools in my basement painting studio. I complained. After all, we built a two-story workshop on our property, why was he cluttering up my space? He admitted that some days, especially in the winter, he couldn't walk the 300 feet to it, so we turned one side of the garage into a smaller work area for him.

He was the one who always dragged the cans of garbage to the street every two weeks. Now he added a hook on his truck bumper and towed them to the curb.

I thought he was clever, not dying.

Referred by his regular doctor, we went to see an oncologist because of his increasing fatigue. The receptionist greeted each arriving patient by name.

"I never want to go to a doctor where everybody knows me by name," he said when we were home. That degree of familiarity meant you were seriously sick. And he was. After weeks of tests, blood work, and biopsies, he was diagnosed with a disease of the bone marrow. I look it up online, average life expectancy is 60 months. I try to wrap my mind around that number: 60 months, five years. He is 58 years old.

He beat the average and lived another eight years; of course, by then all the nurses at the hospital where he got his transfusions knew him by name.

He participated in multiple clinical trials, he never complained, but continued to work as an industrial designer building product prototypes for large corporations. When we first moved to Connecticut, he joined the local volunteer fire department. "You're too old," I scolded. He wouldn't be a firefighter, he said, but an EMT, emergency medical technician. He'd help with 911 calls: car accidents, falls, heart attacks, and the like. And he did, until the end.

I thought he was indomitable; we would grow old together. For years I have lain awake nights reliving every choice, every decision, searching for anything that could have changed the outcome.

When he went on a call, patients would ask, "Will I die?" He'd answer, "Not while you're with me." I repeated that mantra in my head as if it were a magical incantation that could keep him safe at each doctor's visit, with every clinical trial and new drug, until it didn't.

Not while you're with me.

*I will never be afraid again*, I think after he dies. After all, the worst thing that could happen, did happen. And aside from a minor scare over a breast lump, or a stray bump in the night, it's true.

# The End

"I can't breathe," he says. His chest hurts. I run to the nurse's station; something is terribly wrong. They hurry back to his room. The catheter that runs from his groin to his heart has shifted. They throw the monitor on his bed and, running together, we wheel his bed down the hall. They leave me outside the double doors of the surgery.

I retreat to an empty hallway and sit alone. This area of the hospital is quiet. I am alone with the knowledge that he is dying. Of course, we have both known it for months, but rarely spoken, not faced but felt in my gut, in my bones.

We talked once about moving. I suggested selling the house and moving to a condo. It would be easier for him without the stairs and yard. He said I could do that after he was dead, which made me furious. Did he have any idea what a cruel thing that was to say? I couldn't bear the thought of living without him.

The day I called 911, he didn't want to go to the hospital. "I'll die there," he said. My response was "If we don't go, you'll die right here, on the floor."

We went, and he did die there. Not right away; they tried what they could. But the damage the disease had done to his body was too great. All his internal organs were breaking down, and there was nothing more they could do.

He is moved to a hospice floor. I call my youngest son to come say goodbye to his father. He does, and then I send him home. I don't want him to see his father die. Friends come and sit with him. They give me a recliner chair so I can stay in his room. I bring his favorite CDs, especially George Jones, and play them for him.

During all those visits to the doctors, I would joke, "not while you're with me!" Now I am alone with the reality that he is dying.

I sit in the dark rocking back and forth wailing, sobbing, snot and tears slicking my face. I understand that my life as I knew it is over. He is leaving me, forever. I will be alone.

When I can cry no more, I wipe my face, stand, and go back to wait outside the surgery.

I have never cried again.

# Working Girl

# Jack of All Trades

I am a dilettante with the attention span of a newt. I bore easily, have infinite curiosity, and love the new and shiny. That's what I learned from working.

My first job was babysitting, which I did once. The infant screamed the entire time, and nothing I tried — warm bottle, rocking, crooning — would make it stop. More successful were stints as a stablehand, slopping out stalls and exercising polo ponies.

I, along with my boyfriend-husband-to-be, worked after school collating booklets at a classmate's father's print shop. In college, I worked as a waitress at a busy local diner, where I learned how to multitask, carry six cups of coffee in one hand and avoid the grabby hands of the cook.

I spent a year on a kibbutz in Israel where I got to do lots of jobs; I was a *Peh'cock* (the Hebrew word for "cork"), filling in for workers on vacation, women on maternity leave, or where a task needed extra hands, like seasonal fruit picking.

The kibbutz grew a variety of fruits. Standing on a ladder that I moved from tree to tree, I picked lemons and grapefruits with a small tool that fit over my thumb to cut the stem (and gave me blisters until my skin toughened). Up close, the fragrance was wonderful.

Grapes are grown on low arbors; I'd pick bunches and put them in a sack hanging from my shoulder. There was no shade, so the picking started before dawn when the grapes were icy cold (and delicious; I'd snack as I worked). By noon the sun was brutal, the grapes sticky.

I packed chickens in crates to sell at the market, a nasty job. I was given tall black rubber boots to wear in the chicken houses where the droppings on the floor were inches deep and there were always snakes.

When I opened the door of the coop, the hens would cluster in the back. I'd reach in and grab one by the leg and drag it out, repeating until I held at least three, each hanging by a leg in one fist, while I captured another in my free hand.

I tried to be gentle, but the hens objected strenuously and would reach up and peck at my hands, drawing blood, at which point I'd swing my arm and smack their heads against my boot, stunning them, until I could get them into the crate. I hated that job, and the chickens.

In the kibbutz kitchen, I helped cook three meals a day for more than 300 people. I chopped vegetables, peeled potatoes, plucked and prepared chickens (chickens, again!). These tasks required constant soaking and rinsing of my hands, but ironically, instead of dry cracked skin, all that chicken fat left them smooth and supple.

I cleaned the public bathhouse and toilets, scrubbing fixtures and washing the floors in the low cement buildings with tin roofs and separate entrances for men and women. The peacocks that roamed the property would clatter about on the roofs as I worked.

At the children's house, I fetched meals from the kitchen, set out breakfast, snacks and lunch for the children, and cleaned up afterward. When they went down for naps in the afternoons, I polished their shoes and washed the floors.

I worked in the laundry, a wonderful, if solitary, job. Kibbutz members would drop off their bags of laundry and I would use the industrial-size washers and dryers for the clothes, hanging sheets on outside clotheslines. I developed a rhythm: bend over, take a sheet from the basket, pin one end with a clothespin kept in a large pocket in the apron I wore, push the line forward, clip the other end of the sheet, bend over, pick up, clip ... and on and on, for hours at a time. Sometimes the shift would be overnight, and I would read a book, lying on the giant piles of bagged clean clothes while the dryers hummed and turned.

The kibbutz had an Olympic-size pool, and with my American lifesaving certificate, I was occasionally tapped as a lifeguard. Sounds cushy? It was not. Half the residents were from England, and they swam poorly, if at all; they required constant vigilance. The other Anglo-Saxon pool-goers, from Australia and New Zealand, swam like otters. The French, stray Germans, and other residents fell somewhere in between. I developed a gorgeous tan and stress headaches.

Best of all, I learned to drive a tractor. One of my happiest memories is plowing a field. Starting with drunken swerves and uneven furrows, I eventually mastered both the driving and plowing (a two-handed process). Looking back at the dark, straight lines of turned-over soil, I thought, *I will stay here forever.* I didn't, but that's another story.

On Friday evenings, the *Siddur*, general manager, would post a bulletin board with the work positions listed across the top. Jobs included picking fruit, kitchen duty, assembly tasks in the small factory, the children's houses, and laundry, and down the side, the names of the adult kibbutz members.

Many jobs were regular, with few changes, like herding the kibbutz's flock of sheep. Doris, whose room was next to mine in the small, low building we shared, was a shepherd, and I could smell her when she came home at the end of the day.

Because I was only a guest, albeit a working one, my name was on the bottom of the board and my assignments shifted all the time. The workweek itself was six days. It took a while for that realization to sink in; there was no "weekend," only the 24 hours of the Friday evening Jewish Sabbath, to Saturday night.

One day I decided not to work. I don't remember why, but on that day, I played hooky. I didn't go to the communal dining hall for meals, I just hung out. When I returned to the hall the next day, my name had been erased from the board. I fled back to my room, mortified and ashamed.

On the third day, I went to the *Siddur* and begged him to put me back on the roster. I offered no excuse but apologized and said it would not happen again. He listened, nodded, and put my name back (I think that's when he assigned me to clean the public toilets for a week).

In a society where every able-bodied member of the community works, to not contribute is to be a pariah.

The other enduring lesson I gained from that experience was a respect for work itself. In the kibbutz, no one came to clean your house, repair your plumbing, or cook your food. If something needed to be fixed, it was done by members of the community. There were no good jobs or bad jobs, there were just tasks that needed doing, and someone had to do them.

I was married for a very long time to a man who could make and fix almost anything. He was truly a "Jack of all trades." He made furniture, chandeliers, fountains, a fishpond, a treehouse, and playscapes for our sons.

He even built me a chicken coop. Finally! Chickens I could love.

# *Skin Deep*

I read somewhere that by 2025, white people will be a minority in this country. That reality upsets a lot of people, but not me. After all, as a Jew in America, I've always been in the minority, but you can't tell my religion by my looks. If I keep my mouth shut, I could easily pass as a Christian.

Race is a whole other thing. The color of one's skin is a dead giveaway. Jewish or not, I've always been part of the white majority.

I first understood what being a minority felt like more than 40 years ago. After graduating from college, I worked on an anthropological research grant in Newark, New Jersey, a city that was, and probably still is, majority black. The job required that all employees get a drug test at the local hospital, which was across the street from the Quonset hut that housed our research study. My boss told me to go and get it done. It was summer, and the hospital waiting room was packed with 30 to 40 people, mostly standing, and no air conditioning. I signed in, found a vacant spot against a wall, and waited.

Sweating and uncomfortable, I was acutely aware that I was the only white person there. My anxiety grew: what if they didn't call me in turn but skipped over me? If they did, should I complain? Make a scene? Not say anything?

Is that what black people experience? Every day? When I see a person of color trying to get the attention of a sales clerk, or when they're alone in front of an all-white group, I wonder if they worry about sounding dumb, or difficult, or worst of all, being invisible.

White people don't usually worry about being invisible (old people are the ones unseen, but that's a topic for another time). I think white fear is that of retribution; afraid that when those who have been oppressed have power, they will retaliate and treat white people as badly as they were once treated.

Payback time, baby!

I remember that crowded waiting room. My anxiety was unfounded: the black hospital staff didn't treat me any differently because I was white —

they were as short-tempered and unpleasant to me as they were to every other person in the room.

As a future minority, I expect some people will be rude to me, some will not. After all, there are stupid, mean, and ignorant people of every race in every generation. As long as they're not rounding me up and putting me in a cattle car heading to a concentration camp, I'm prepared to follow the Judaic dictum, "What you yourself hate, don't do to your neighbor." (I believe Jesus said the same thing, but he's not my go-to guy; and I think maybe Hillel the Elder said it first.)

The mechanic who repairs my car, the local elected official, the kid who mows my lawn, my Trump-voting hairdresser, the sales clerk at Walmart, I treat them all as I would like to be treated.

Is that enough? No, but it's a start. Notwithstanding my good intentions (path to hell and all that ...), I am still guilty of the mote in my own eye.

For 25 years I've lived in a historic building with broadsides from the early 1900s adorning the walls. These posters announced social events in this building and used terms such as "Coon songs," and "Darkies," to describe the entertainment. I saw them as quaint, albeit racist, vestiges of a bygone age, and never thought about the impact on black visitors to my home until a gay friend (who knows about discrimination firsthand), pointed out to me that if I walked into a building that had such posters but instead of those offending words, it spoke of "Jew" or "Kike" songs, how would I feel?

The posters are gone. But my inability to see my own complicity still stings; I have more work to do.

# Road Warrior

$A$ workshop by David King touting sales as a great career for women convinced me to enter that profession at age 40.

I remember him saying, "In sales, you will meet more people in a year than most people meet in a lifetime." I found that notion thrilling beyond belief and never looked back.

The first job I interviewed for was in Newark, at a sheet metal distributor. It was an inside sales job, working at a desk. In his pitch to hire me, the boss assured me that an "outside" sales job was not for a nice girl like me. Here, I'd save on clothes as I could wear jeans to work (I'd be climbing on and off trucks all day, measuring the rolls of steel), while as an outside rep, besides the cost of clothing, I would be "driving all over, forced to use gas station rest stops, and eat at crummy diners."

I asked to see where I would work, and he took me for a tour. The place was grungy, the carpets stained black with steel dust. The breakroom consisted of stacks of bottled water, a few small tables and chairs, a tiny refrigerator, a sink, and an outdated pinup calendar on the wall.

The three salesmen sat together in a smoke-filled windowless room, where the empty desk that would be mine faced a burly, shirt-sleeved man whose desk sported a large ceramic frog leaning back with his front legs behind his head and a huge erection. I couldn't figure out what its purpose was: to store rubber bands? A conversation starter? Did he think it was a piece of art?

I thanked the boss for the opportunity but turned the job down — not because of the frog, or the filth, but because he said he'd like to hire a woman, "to tone the place up." He didn't say "clean," and I truly believe he thought merely having a woman on site would make the men change, get their act together.

Would the guy with the frog remove it? I doubted it. And why would a nice girl like me work in such a setting? As a footnote, I saw that same desk ornament years later while visiting San Francisco. My husband and were strolling on Fisherman's Wharf, and there they were: row upon row of reclining frogs with large erections decorating a booth selling tchotchkes to tourists. Who knew?

I turned down other jobs: a trade association for CPAs; a publishing company; and then there was an opportunity to sell cleaning supplies to corporations. Thinking maybe I was setting my sights too high and was being too picky, I considered it, but before accepting, I asked to go out in the field with their best salesperson. So I spent a day in the field with Joe.

Joe mostly cold-called, that is, he didn't have appointments but would drop in at a company, chat with the receptionist, and ask her to call the purchasing manager, who maybe (though frequently not), would come out into the busy lobby with corporate visitors coming and going, and Joe would give his sales pitch.

This scene was repeated all day, at multiple offices. At the end of the day, I had learned a lot and I could see why Joe was excellent at what he did: he was likeable, hardworking, and most important, he had a hide of steel to handle public rejection multiple times each day, every day. I thanked him for his time and courtesy and declined the job offer.

This wasn't the idea of sales that David King had inspired me to pursue, but all these trial balloons helped me figure out exactly what kind of salesperson

I wanted to be. I didn't want to sell a commodity, like cleaning supplies, where the deciding factor was always going to be price.

I didn't want to conduct sales standing in a crowded corporate lobby; I wanted to have appointments with presidents, or VPs of manufacturing, people who had budgets and the power to make decisions, and meet them in their offices in a local territory.

So, I became an outside sales rep, a "road warrior."

In the early '80s, women in outside sales were not that common — and if they were, they sold "female-oriented products," like advertising or cosmetics. I got a job as an outside rep for a research company that sold information services to senior executives, data that helped them make decisions, like should they build the new manufacturing plant in Ireland or Germany, or what was the market size for a widget they were planning to make.

From there, I moved on to selling management training to executives, mostly men, of manufacturing companies.

My husband was not thrilled. He'd heard stories of marriages that had failed because the woman was in "outside sales." I pointed out that if I wanted to be unfaithful, I could screw the mailman, I didn't have to drive thousands of miles to do it. But I did make sure that I arranged my schedule so that I was home every night.

In those years, there was a certain advantage to being a woman selling in a male-dominated environment. When I called for an appointment, I usually got one. I was like a "talking dog," a novelty act, and I'd get invited in so they could see what I looked like. Once in, they found it was hard to get rid of me; I was relentless in pursuit of a sale. Persistent Judith, that was me.

My car was my travelling office. The passenger seat was littered with water bottles, tampons, snacks, my briefcase, and pocketbook, along with state and local maps (there were no cellphones or Google). My crates of sales materials were in the trunk.

At the time I owned a used Toyota Corolla without air-conditioning. I frequently arrived at my destination soggy and damp, sponging myself off in the company bathroom before I met with the prospect.

Outside sales was hard work and long days. I put hundreds of miles on my car every week between our home in New Jersey and my territory, which covered New Jersey, Westchester County, Connecticut, and Rhode Island. Most of the trips themselves were uneventful, but there were scary moments, like getting a flat late one rainy night on the Interstate. I limped off the highway outside Bridgeport to a gas station where the attendant in the booth stared out at me through his bulletproof glass but didn't move to help. A kindly man who was getting gas changed my tire (I recall he used a five-inch switchblade knife to pry off the rim, while I held my umbrella over him).

The most memorable misadventure was getting caught in a flood in the McClellan Street underpass, a low-lying part of the road in the industrial section of Newark, known to flood (just not to me, apparently). My car hit a pothole and got stuck in the middle of the underpass, the water rose rapidly, I was trying not to panic. I was alone, cars that came down the road and saw my car settling deeper and deeper into the rising water turned around and drove away.

I had no idea how deep the water was, it was winter, it was getting dark, plus I was wearing a heavy, ankle-length coat with a hood. How would I wade through the water? Should I take the coat off to escape? Would I freeze to death if I didn't drown?

And then ... a miracle. A giant garbage truck appeared in my rearview mirror. Just like in a Western, where the hero rides down and rescues the maiden by scooping her up onto his saddle, the truck driver drove into the underpass, came alongside, opened my passenger door, reached down, and lifted me up onto his lap and drove us out.

I cried out, "Wait, wait, I forgot to lock my car!"

He laughed and said, "Lady, nobody's coming to steal your car."

Sales helped me become the person I am today. It fed my curiosity, my most enduring trait. Sale or no sale, I learned something on every call: plant managers would always offer to show me their operation, and so I learned about the special reflective paint with which the lines on highways are marked, how spaghetti is made (I had imagined it grew in fields and was cut with a scythe).

I watched Hispanic women use large paddles to stir giant vats filled with red liquid that would be turned into high-end lipsticks. I saw the assembly line where liquid was converted into a powder and packaged as detergent.

In my long sales career, I became a repository of a little bit about a whole lot of things. At a party, I can talk for five minutes on almost any topic. That's me: wide and shallow.

# Arty Farty

In plugging the gaps in my memoir, I have neglected to write about my artistic endeavors. A glaring oversight, as I spend a good part of my days doing something "creative."

I resist the title, "artist." When asked "what do I do?" my typical answer is, "I paint." The answer to the next question of what do I paint? "Anything that's not moving."

If that sounds too cute by half, it's true. I can paint almost anything. I can produce realistic portraits, landscapes, or florals, though I prefer to paint abstracts. I've painted windows, Styrofoam snowman, large sheets of Plexiglas, Tyvek banners, mirror frames, garden accessories, trays, bowls, chairs, tables, and other miscellaneous pieces of furniture.

Long ago, I was an art student at Syracuse University. I flunked out in my second year (too many men, too little time is my glib explanation for my failure). I returned to painting after working as a social anthropologist, followed by 25 years in corporate sales, starting when we moved to Connecticut with a class at Rhode Island School of Design's decorative painting program. There I made lifelong friends and learned many painting techniques using layering and patterns.

I think I was heading to developing a craft. But the crafters whose work I've seen at shows demonstrate an attention to detail and a consistent technique, a way of working that they can replicate again and again. I possess few of those skills and none of the required patience. I'm also not good in talking about what I do.

For someone who was so successful in outside sales and certainly has the gift of gab, I am uncomfortable trying to articulate my "process." Most artist statements that I read feel overwrought and pretentious. Most often, my painting is designed to solve a problem.

Sometimes it's as basic as painting a canvas to fill an empty wall in my home. Or I need a piece of furniture to hold a large potted plant. As a road warrior, an outside sales rep, I drove thousands of miles each year in several adjacent states. During the work week I would pull off on the side of the road at a yard sale, find an interesting piece, throw it in my car and continue on my route. At the end of the day, I'd lug it home where David would clean it up, reglue and repair it and then I'd paint the piece to fit the spot. On the weekends, I'd hit auctions and flea markets with like-minded friends or my willing husband.

My greatest pleasure is simply playing with color. Usually when in my studio, I listen to music. I dance around my studio, waving my brush aloft as I blast out Delbert McClintock, Leon Redbone, Willie Nelson, and other favorites. It is more than a hobby and less than a business; it feels more like a compulsion. (If it were a hobby, it wouldn't be such hard work, and if it were a business, I would only paint what customers want.)

It is challenging, intense, absorbing, and frequently frustrating as my hand refuses to create what my mind imagines. My standard is unreachable. I paint dreck (that's Yiddish for shit), and then suddenly it comes together into something that pleases me. Of course, it would be great if I stopped then — but that's not always the case, and back it goes to awful.

There are days when I feel all I do is waste paint. But not always.

I look at completed pieces and wonder: how did I make something so beautiful? It feels completely out of my control, I cannot replicate what I've done before. And yet, I persevere.

# Who You Calling an Artist?

I know many creative people. Some are painters, a few sculptors, and ceramists. Most wouldn't use the "A" word; some say "hobby," to describe what they do. I think they are making art.

My neighbor, Bob, has model trains set up in his basement. He has a friend in a neighboring town, who has a similar setup — more elaborate than Bob's, it sprawls over a huge area of the room's square footage, about chest high. It is a not-so-small town, with factories, a downtown, residential areas, bridges spanning a river, a harbor, and much, much more.

My brother-in-law also was an aficionado. He had two elaborate scenes: a winter landscape and a summer one. After my sister died, he sold the house and it was all taken down and the thousands of pieces of trains, tracks, trees, and buildings sold.

Bob's setup is of a summer in Maine, as he states with dead seriousness: "It's always summer in Maine."

Then there's Carol, another neighbor, who would blush and demur if you called her an artist. This year at Hanukkah, she brought me a platter of homemade cookies. Large and small menorahs, dreidels, and Stars of David iced in blues, golds, silver, and white. They were so beautiful I was reluctant to set them out to be eaten.

I recall once seeing a hideous display in a rural front yard made up of a whirligig, a large gnome, and four wooden cutout flowers. The whole arrangement was garish and crude. But what struck me was the clear desire to make something beautiful; I doubt the property owner set out to create an ugly display. It was art — maybe bad art, but art, nonetheless.

Model trains is obviously a popular hobby, as is baking. But there are thousands of others (check out Wikipedia — it will make your head spin). Stamp, coin, insect, or mineral collecting, flower arranging, quilting, birdwatching, rug hooking, axe throwing, whale watching, and others more obscure, like the small framed "Noah's Ark" that I purchased years ago at a craft show, an exquisite example of the art of "Scherenschnitte," or paper cutting.

Adherents collect catalogs, read magazines dedicated to their particular activity, belong to clubs of similarly inclined others, and attend shows of like-minded people. For many, I expect, it is much more than a hobby. It's a passion and each in its own way, a kind of art.

The instinct for beauty is powerful. With or without training or specialized schooling, I think everybody has it. Some people study for years, some achieve recognition, most do not, but no matter their background, their enjoyment and self-fulfillment are just as strong.

In creating our home, besides having David build everything on my "Honey Do" list, the desire to make it beautiful influenced every roadside purchase, every antique auction, every yard sale or flea market find. I like that in every corner of the house there is something interesting to see, and each piece has a history.

Here's my ideal job: I'm the "Lone Ranger of beauty," sort of an interior designer without the credentials. I'd go around making people's houses more beautiful. They'd invite me in, and I'd show them how to make their houses more interesting, more attractive — a little paint here, move a piece there — and then I'd get on my horse, tip my hat, and ride off ... .

Will my children want my collections? Will my treasures fit their lifestyle or taste? Probably not. Maybe a piece here or there, but not all of it. They will create their own collections, their own heirlooms. My treasures will be sold, probably at an auction, and strangers will take away pieces of my life, and not even know it.

# Friendship

# Men I
# Didn't Sleep With

I never want to be the kind of woman who talks trash about her exes. Instead, I'd rather write about the men I deliberately rejected, the men I didn't sleep with.

There were two buddies in college, Jim and Bob, who are friends to this day; I doubt that would be true if I had bedded them. There was the drawling Southern boy, Thomas Gregory, who gave me a kitten (forbidden in my dorm).

There was Don from a neighboring college when I was a young and naïve freshman. He was a really sweet guy. If I had been older or smarter, I would have held onto him. I wish I could remember his last name, but it is lost along with that of an older student during summer school I had a crush on.

After I flunked out of college, my family didn't know what to do with me, and so shipped me off to Israel, where several of my mother's siblings lived, where I worked on a kibbutz, learned Hebrew, and eventually married an Israeli (another of my not-so-smart decisions) and returned to the United States (read *The Pasha*).

Fast forward 18 months: I am divorced, the mother of a baby boy, back living in my parents' apartment and needing a job. A cousin working at a university gets me an interview, and I am hired as an undefined assistant in the public relations department, working in lower Manhattan.

There I am, a young woman, somewhat shell-shocked and vulnerable at the turn my life has taken, dropped into this department of three men. Over the course of the next year, two of them pursued me sexually. Today it would be considered wildly inappropriate and likely sexual harassment. Back then, I assumed it was my fault.

The first was Stan, one of the two copy-writers. A tall, affable 40-something fellow, he was easygoing and friendly. He would sit on the edge of my desk and tell me funny stories. One night we both ended up working late and when we were alone, he cornered me, dragging me onto his lap, trying to kiss and fondle me.

I was terrified that I was going to be raped, but I managed to persuade him that while I thought he was a great guy, I just "couldn't get involved," my divorce was too fresh, and I was too traumatized. I managed to get away and leave.

Did I tell anyone? No. In those days, it never occurred to me that this was unacceptable behavior. There was nothing in the employee handbook for such situations.

Did I encourage Stan? Did I flirt or act seductive, or suggestive? I didn't think so. Or was just the fact that I was a young, unattached woman that allowed Stan to think that I was fair game? We continued to work together, and he never propositioned me again. But he was also less friendly, and while I missed the camaraderie, it made work easier.

The second man was the boss, a balding Orthodox Jew in his early 50s; he smoked a pipe, wore a yarmulke, and rarely smiled. The offices were cramped. Initially my desk was placed up against his in a tiny alcove; we worked facing each other across the expanses of the two desktops.

My first task was to type out congratulatory telegrams from dignitaries to a new member of the university's board of directors, to be handed out at a banquet that evening. I am not a secretary, I don't know shorthand or take dictation, and my six-finger method of typing, while not exactly slow, would never pass muster in any secretarial school.

The boss stood over me while I sat at the manual typewriter and typed out two letters, then he ordered me to "get up," sat down and banged out the remaining letters himself, in seconds. He was an old newspaper guy, and apparently, they all know how to type, and type fast. Mortified, I sat waiting for him to tell me to go home and not to return. But he didn't.

The next day, he set me to work on the production of all our printed promotional pieces. Turns out I was a good proofreader, could spot a typo at 50 paces, and was soon coordinating the myriad flyers and brochures we churned out for the university.

I worked long hours, frequently staying late after others had gone home. The boss would take me out for dinner, then drop me off at the subway when he drove back to the Bronx, where he and his wife lived.

Over time, our interactions became more intimate. I liked and respected him, and I was definitely lonely. We would make out in his car, steaming up the windows. He was more than ready to be unfaithful to his wife.

For me ... after my marriage had been shattered by my husband's philandering, I loved that someone actually wanted me. The situation had all the necessary elements: proximity, opportunity, and desire.

But I couldn't do it. I thought of those young unmarried women who so willingly had sex with my husband, and now I was going to be just like them, doing the same thing to another woman. I didn't want to be that person. So the nascent affair ended.

I never slept with another woman's husband. My childhood boyfriend, David, came back into my life, we married, and I never even looked at another man.

That is, until the Israeli.

You'd think after my poor choice of a first husband, I'd avoid Israelis like the plague. I'm in my late 40s, I've been married for some time, working as an outside sales rep selling supervisory training to companies.

I call on a VP of manufacturing, an Israeli with a full head of black hair, a rumbling deep voice and terrific smile. I find him very attractive and enjoy flirting with him when he sits and observes the training classes his supervisors are taking. We have follow-up meetings about the training and eventually, he invites me out to lunch.

I accept, with a pretty good idea of where this is going. I don't see how I can pretend to be surprised that he suggests infidelity, so instead, as we are finishing eating, I take a deep breath and tell him I'd been thinking of having an affair.

He listens eagerly as I explain that I'd been thinking about it and so I told my husband, David (at this point his expression changes from lust to dumbstruck), and that what I really wanted was "the *feeling* of an affair": the breathless excitement, the eager anticipation. So my husband and I "talked about ways to put some of that feeling back into our marriage, but that I would never actually have an affair, because it would hurt my husband, and I would never want to do that," and does he understand?

He rouses from his shock and admits he does. We talk some more, he about his marriage, me about mine. We finish lunch, and as we stand outside the restaurant he asks if perhaps our two couples could be friends? I say no, he "is much too attractive, it would never work." That was a salve for his ego and the truth.

Today, I'm an old woman, and as such, I'm pretty much invisible. Men no longer hit on me. They call me "Ma'am" and treat me like their favorite grandmother. But I still occasionally flirt. That playful repartee between a man and woman is a lovely thing, and I don't intend to give it up.

# My Bestie

She would hate that I'm writing about her. That's the first thing you should know.

We are an odd combo, as different as "chalk and cheese." She is a sunny day; I am cloudy with a chance of showers.

We are Mutt and Jeff. She is spider-like, round middle, with long arms and legs. I am an ant — compact body, low to the ground. She is a fair-skinned blonde and avoids the sun. In summer I turn nut brown.

We are both voracious readers, with large vocabularies (part of our compatibility), but she likes happy endings, I prefer grit. She mixes her metaphors, saying "water under the dam," or "water over the bridge," which make no sense, but are quite funny.

She has many domestic skills like sewing (she can make a man's suit), and she is a superb baker. I am a more intuitive and creative cook, but baking is a science and requires discipline and exactitude — her strengths, not mine.

She is patient, calm, and kind. Her last job, at a local large hospital, involved meeting with former patients, and soliciting donations. She excelled because she would take the time, not just doing her research, but because she genuinely enjoyed spending an afternoon sipping tea with a garrulous old person. I was in outside sales, so our tasks were basically the same: persuading people to part with their money; hers was a more genteel extraction.

By nature, she is a happy person. She lives in the emotional middle, "moderation in all things." I go to extremes. Maybe it comes from her Protestant middle-class, Norwegian ancestry, with none of the drama of my wandering Jew forebearers.

We met in a suburb of Chicago, where my husband and I had moved after marrying, and he took a job as a product designer with American Can Company. We settled in a garden apartment complex in the middle of nowhere. I joked that a tornado — which were common in our area — would sweep us away and no one would notice until we didn't pay the next month's rent. Winters were brutal, summers scorching.

They had boxes of books. That was the first thing I noticed when she, her husband, and an infant daughter moved in across the courtyard not long after we did.

She would put her daughter in a baby carriage and, balancing a laundry basket on it, walk to the laundromat in the small strip mall about a half mile from our complex. Our apartment had a stacking washer and dryer. I offered her the use of them; she declined.

We had two cars, they had one, which her husband took daily to work. I drove a small Sunbeam Imp that my spouse had driven in competitive road rallies back East. It was small, compact; a baby fit perfectly in the long, low well behind the back seat. I offered her the use of it. She declined.

She thought I was loud and pushy, I thought she was aloof and cold. Each saw the other as an alien being.

One hot summer day, I saw her sweating — not a ladylike glow as in the adage, "Horses sweat, men perspire, ladies' glow"— but *schvitzing* like a horse, like me. That changed everything.

See? Mutt and Jeff. And still, we became friends.

She is the person I called from the hospital when my husband was dying. She immediately drove from three states away to stay with me. When I am anxious, lonely, or blue — that's who I call.

When I face big decisions, I turn to her for advice, as her judgment is sensible and trustworthy. She wants what's best for me, as I do for her.

Together, we have been through most of life's traumas: illness, grief, and death. We have also shared in innumerable moments of happiness, joy, and delight. When we were both married, the four of us would vacation together. She was the one who would usually pick the destination and plan all the activities.

Now she and I take trips together and are the best of travel companions. That's huge. If you've ever traveled with someone whose rhythms of waking, dining, and entertainment are completely different from yours, you know how rare it is to find a compatible travel buddy.

From the beginning, we established a tradition of our two couples eating dinner together twice a week. We'd alternate houses, and after dinner, we'd put the kids to bed (my husband strung up a baby monitoring system so we could hear if they cried or woke up) and we'd play board games or cards.

We raised our families together. We share our talents and help make each other's home beautiful. Together, we believe we can do anything.

We created a support network for each other that has endured to this day.

Long ago, we decided that nothing would end our friendship, but that meant when one was unhappy with the other, it had to be talked out and worked through. We've done that successfully for more than 50 years.

Recently she called and told me she'd finally had a long-awaited appointment with a geriatrics specialist and, after multiple tests, she was given a diagnosis of MCI — mild cognitive impairment. Being who she is, she accepts it with equanimity. I grieve — for her, for us, for a future that we probably won't have (although to talk about the future when one is in one's 80s is in itself wishful thinking or delusional).

Sure, I've noticed her increasing forgetfulness, her inability to complete a thought, her issues with balance (which our thrice weekly exercise class is helping to mitigate). We are aging differently. No surprise there. But the physical changes are becoming more obvious when we walk together. I used to trot to match her longer stride; not anymore.

What remains, and hopefully will until the end, is our abiding love for each other. That we continue to be attuned to the other's hopes and fears, ready with a supporting word, a caring gesture, and a commiserating shoulder to cry on is a given.

It is enough.

# Fag Hag

There's a lot of stereotypical ideas of friendship between a straight woman and a gay man. She's called names, implying that she's too unattractive to get a man of her own, or that she needs someone to control, or he only uses her as a "beard," so people won't assume he's gay.

None of them explain my 35-year friendship with one particular gay man.

We met over the phone. I was a brand-new New Jersey sales rep for a Connecticut publishing firm that sold professional newsletters and motivational materials to businesses. He was a computer nerd working in the home office in the eastern part of the state. I called needing territory information; he was helpful.

When I first visited the office, I went to find him. He sat in a tiny cubicle, slight of build, handsome, and charming. His desk was devoid of personal mementos, no photos of a girlfriend, children, buddies, nothing but an ornate desk clock, a parting gift it turned out, from some previous job. I thought, he's gay; I was right, but that was only confirmed months later.

Whenever I came to headquarters, we'd go for lunch in a place that overlooked the New London harbor, or we'd have dinner at a Greek/Lebanese restaurant that we both liked; we discovered we were both foodies. I told him about David, he told me little, other than mentioning "the person he lived with."

It was at dinner one evening, when he once again used that elusive answer, that I asked him point blank: "What's that person's name?"

He sat very still, and then said his name. "Don't you feel better?" I asked, he laughed and agreed.

After that, it got easier. We talked freely, finding common ground in our shared passions of gardening, cooking, and antiquing. We became friends and he trusted me enough to open his world and life to me.

In 1988 it was dangerous for a gay person to be "out." Killings were not uncommon, and it wasn't until Matthew Shepard's murder in 1998 that the tide of public understanding began to change, albeit at a snail's pace. Today, while there is more acceptance and more openness, the number of hate crimes have increased as well. Now it's not just individual gay men under attack, but crowds of them, at clubs, schools, bars; hate is making a comeback in America.

I am aware of the irony in not naming him here. But he was, and remains, guarded, private, always coiled, ready for insult — "pansy," "queer," "homo." I will not willingly expose him to more of the same.

Before I met him, I casually used such slurs as well, without connecting to the pain it could cause. I thought I was cool, sophisticated. I cringe at the memory.

I didn't know any out gay people. I made assumptions, judging people by mannerisms, or stereotypes. Because of our friendship, I have met and befriended many homosexuals, many of whom look a lot like the straight men I know, only with better taste and more wit.

———————

He's much more mellow these days. He's happily married and can be openly himself, but he has not forgotten any of that, and why would he? Recently he was called "faggot" at the local market, and casual homophobia is still rampant, as he notes, "even among people I consider friends. They make judgments that someone must be gay, because of the way he acts or talks. They joke and say, things like, 'that's so gay'." People stare when he and his husband go out to eat.

When I was promoted to sales administration, I had to spend more time in the home office. I would drive up on Tuesday or Wednesday, go home on Friday. I stayed at a Holiday Inn on I-95. Always the same room, overlooking a retention basin where mallards swam among the reeds (was that the inspiration for our pond?), and the front desk kept my feather pillow for me from week to week.

My friend and I shared our lives. Sometimes I stayed overnight with him and his partner at their old farmhouse. After work we would do repairs or garden together. Sometimes David would drive up as well, and the four of us would go out to dinner, visit tag sales and work on their house over the weekend.

He and I wallpapered their dining room. David rebuilt the sagging columns on their porch. They gave us their old tractor when we moved to Connecticut. They held an annual Christmas party every year; I would arrive early and we'd cook for two days.

When we moved to Connecticut, he was the one who designed our gardens and did the digging and planting.

We have gardened and cooked together for more than 30 years. He helps with every party I host; I can't imagine having an event without him. He prefers to stay in the kitchen, but since that's where people always tend to congregate, he gets to socialize at a level he's comfortable with. He usually goes home once dinner is served.

We share a perverse sense of humor.

He looks much younger than he is, always has. When we go shopping together, people sometimes mistake us for mother and son, not unreasonable, as he is 17 years younger than I. He gleefully milks it, asking me, "What do you think, Mother?" and "Watch your step, Mother!"

In return, I wrote him a fictitious job recommendation that spoke about his great strides in recovery with AA, and his overcoming the "unfortunate recent arrest."

He is kind, hardworking, and generous. He can also be brutally vicious and cold. Fights with him are frightening things, but somehow, we always talk it through, make up, and never give up on the friendship.

There is the family you are born in to, and then there's the family you create: the people who know you, love you, accept you, and are there through the good times and the bad.

That's him.

# Visit to Another Planet

I have returned from a weekend spent with friends in Maine. They lived only briefly in Connecticut, where the wife and I worked together on a municipal study in 2010.

They are not old friends, but people whose company I enjoy. Yet I am continually astounded that that they welcome me into their lives. We come from different planets; nay, solar systems.

The live in a world almost completely foreign to me. Whereas mine is filled with guilt, drama, and family *mishugas* (craziness), theirs has none of that. They exist in a universe of common-sense rules: you want something, work for it. You commit to something, do it.

They are loving but firm, generous but not extravagant. Frugal, but not cheap. Their home is tasteful and comfortable, but not showy. When they built it, they eschewed air conditioning, finding Maine's climate not so torrid, and satisfied with opening windows and turning on ceiling fans. One of my paintings that I gifted them is framed, and I see it as soon as I walk in their front door.

Most long-married couples I know resemble "The Bickersons." Spouses picking on each other over the multiple small differences in how they navigate their world. My Downeasters do none of that.

The husband, a tall, lanky engineer by training, is detail-oriented, and over the past six years has become an avid beekeeper. If encouraged, he can talk at length about the lives of bees and their importance in the environment.

He has the sense of humor of a teenager, and he likes to tease — but without malice. One year, at Christmas, they brought me a case of Two Buck Chuck wine from Trader Joe's. The husband had made new labels for each bottle: A picture of Connecticut's governor with the label, "Wine for Everyone," and similar jibes.

His wife, the mother of four accomplished grown children, is a nurse by training. Organized and competent, she excels at everything she applies her hand to. Both retired, they volunteer with multiple causes. They are kind, and loving to each other.

I take ill the first evening of my stay. We have driven to a nearby town that has pickleball courts, and after I play one game the slight pain in my right abdomen that I had noticed after dinner becomes unbearable. I can't play anymore; I can barely stand.

The wife packs me in her car and drives me to a hospital. There, we wait in the ER for six hours. By the time I am examined, have a CAT scan, blood drawn, vitals taken, the pain has subsided. They find nothing.

There are few things worse than being far from home and feeling awful. A horrible ordeal, that finally ends when we return to the house at 2 a.m. I am the guest from hell. (I can only imagine what the hospital bill will be.)

The husband insists that I faked it to avoid losing at pickleball. They gift me a huge box of Raisin Bran the next morning.

I expect never to be invited back. They laugh and tell me, "Don't be silly!"

See what I mean. Who ARE these people?

# News Flash

Today, "Bossy" Judith Podell was again caught giving unsolicited decorating advice to terrified friends trapped in their kitchen. She was finally persuaded to leave with gifts of floral bouquets.

This is not the first time this has occurred. On any given day, she can be found wandering local neighborhoods ringing unsuspecting residents' doorbells. Her technique is cunning in its simplicity. First, gifts of homemade goodies appear, along with cuttings from her garden, or bottles of wine.

Once accepted and invited in, she sets about remaking their home. She persuades, cajoles, bullies, and insists that the victim (homeowner) ditch their carpeting, throw out those curtains, and repaint every room to the colors she has selected.

Resistance is met with eye rolls and pitying glances.

In this latest episode, the local police who responded to the silent alarm sent by the trapped couple said that a warrant was out for her arrest. Meanwhile the police recommended purchasing a stun gun and setting out bear traps around the property's perimeter.

Residents in the area have been advised to lock their doors.

Stay tuned for future updates.

# *Good Intentions*

I am surrounded by friends and neighbors always ready to lend a helping hand. A snowfall brings text messages with offers to come shovel my steps and driveway. I turn them all down as I have a reliable local plow guy who shows up when it's more than four inches deep, and because I prefer to do the hand shoveling myself.

There's something magical about shoveling snow while it's coming down. I'm not talking blizzard, but during a steady snowfall; the air is still, with barely any sound, there's little or no traffic. I bundle up day or night — gloves, a hat or earmuffs, boots, and a warm but not bulky coat — and shovel.

My tool of choice has a bend in the middle. I've used it for years. It's lightweight, wide enough to be effective, but not so big that it's unwieldy.

There's a rhythm to it: reach down, lift, toss, move forward, repeat. I listen to music while I work. My iPhone is in my hip pocket, and I stream a playlist into my hearing aids.

In my early 70s, I hated when tests showed I needed hearing aids. It was the first milepost of being old. But here's the plus about wearing them: I have music with me wherever I go (plus audio books, which is usually what I listen to on long car rides).

Of my several playlists, my longest has 132 songs. It's a variety of tunes I've downloaded from background music heard on TV shows, Broadway musicals, movies, favorite singer's CDs, and old tapes. It includes sentimental old favorites, Don McLean's "Vincent," Arlo Guthrie's "Anytime," folk songs from Peter, Paul, and Mary which take me back to high school and the civil rights movement.

Newer additions include Jimmie Dale Gilmore, Delbert McClintock, Flaco Jimenez, and many more. Some, like Vince Gill's, "Look at Us," make me cry. Mostly, I save upbeat melodies that put me in a good mood. And to those, I dance.

Yes, dancing even when shoveling snow, but also spinning around my living room, late at night, just because. I imagine I am in David's arms, and he is waltzing me around the floor.

I used to complain that David's only flaw was he didn't know how to dance and had no desire to learn. For my 50th birthday, his gift was to take lessons, and for the next 15 years, until he became too sick, we'd go dancing whenever I wanted. He favored the two-step, swing, and the waltz.

Now I have no dance partner. At any social event that has a band, I eye the couples, tapping my foot, and beseech any seated man to give me at least one turn around the floor. It's just another one of the things I miss with David gone.

For all the kind offers of help, what I miss most is company. Companionship. Someone to share with, tell the funny stories of what happened that day, to commiserate when I feel weepy.

The loneliness is most acute at holidays. Not all of them, of course, many of them are spent with good friends or my son and his family. But there are others, like Valentine's Day, where I am nobody's one-and-only, and the void is palpable.

When David died, it was painful to be out in public. In the supermarket or bank, people offered condolences and I could feel their pity, and their silent relief, "I'm glad it's not me."

I think when people learn that a friend has lost their spouse, they cling closer to their other half, if only briefly. Then they forget and move on with their lives, back to the petty bickering, the unspoken grievances, the annoying habits of one's partner that are as much the state of matrimony as sexual pleasure, tolerance, and affection. I suppose I did the same.

Now I envy their twoness. Do they know how lucky they are?

The reality is that no one stays in my small town in eastern Connecticut because of me. They remain or leave based on their family's needs. They choose to move closer to their children, or go somewhere warmer, or where taxes are lower.

I don't begrudge them that choice; it's one David and I would have made together. I am a "nice to have," not a must. On the flip side, I can go wherever I want. Want to live six months of the year in Key West? Spend two months in Tuscany? Go ahead. I could move to be closer to my grandchildren, settle in New Jersey.

Why not? I am untethered and have been now for 15 years. I read about this old woman who lives permanently on ocean liners, continually cruising the world, at a much lower cost than a nursing home.

For now, I'll pull a Scarlett and think about it tomorrow.

Meanwhile, I gratefully accept the gifts of friendship, helping hands, and kindness that are offered.

# Mean Girls

When I was growing up, I wanted to be accepted in the girl cliques that seem to form in adolescence. I was not.

It's not that I didn't have friends. I did. But I wasn't cool. I didn't wear makeup, I didn't giggle.

Fast forward to now, and I'm still trying to fit in with a group of women who are not so different from my fifth-grade classmates.

This time the group was a church book group to which I was initially invited, and then discovered that I was not welcome by several other members. The details don't matter, as after much drama and hurt feelings, it was resolved. I am not in that club but attend the lunch afterward at a local restaurant with some of the women.

What sticks with me is how quickly my initial feelings went from happiness at being included in a group to the same old feelings of rejection — an outsider, unwelcome and unwanted.

Is it the Jewish thing (I am a somewhat rare bird in my community of 10,000 residents), or that old insecurity of not fitting in? Something my mother dismissed out of hand, as she encouraged me to "be myself."

As a girl, I desperately wanted to fit in. But at this advanced age, why does it still smart if I don't?

Women being mean to other women seems to be the cultural norm, and not just in fifth grade. When I was married, I wasn't crazy about my husband having other women friends. I don't think I was alone. Most women seem protective of their relationships — it's alright to have friendships with other couples, but not just with the spouse of the opposite sex.

I speak from experience. When I was widowed, I was *persona non grata* at dinner parties, and other social events where only couples made the cut. I never felt my husband had a desire to stray, but he was a sucker for a "wounded bird," and would be susceptible to a damsel in distress. It was that woman I didn't trust.

Perhaps that's what other women felt about widowed Judy. By now, I'm ancient enough that I am a threat to no one.

When I was young, I preferred the company of men. They weren't catty, bitchy. They don't seem to form the same kinds of cliques (except when gang-raping women). They seemed more noble, more capable of true friendship.

By my 50s, I found women more interesting, and their friendships more meaningful. Sure, when we'd get together, we might talk about our spouses, but I don't recall meanness, or anger, more likely amusement. Was I more mature? Less threatened?

Now, while I still love the company of men, it is my circle of female friends that sustain me. Women who welcome me, embrace me, and want me: Jewish Judy — foul-mouthed, bossy, and all — to be in their company.

# On My Own

# The Art of Isolation

Sometime in early March 2020, the world begins to disappear. Like the frog in the slowly boiling pot of water, the effects at first are imperceptible.

A writing class is cancelled, then the senior center exercise classes stop. A baby shower celebration gone, a niece's wedding is held without guests, a dinner engagement retracted, my book club moves from inperson to Zoom, which no one enjoys.

I hunker down. What else can I do?

I watch a YouTube video on how to make masks. Friends sew me better, prettier ones. I repeat to myself: *You can do this. It's not London during the Blitz, it's not being rounded up in cattle cars and taken to concentration camps or fleeing your country.*

It's just ... sit tight, be careful, wear a mask, and don't get close to anyone. I make the five-hour round trip drive to my son in New Jersey to bring him hand sanitizer and the ingredients to make more. I put the package on his front step, we visit briefly — his neighbor died the night before, they think it was COVID — and drive home. No more visits to see my granddaughters, no sharing a meal. No hugs.

By April, the calendar is blank. Doctor visits become virtual consults, my monthly participation in the Alzheimer study at Yale is halted.

My son says, "You're an artist, make art." But it's hard to concentrate, and fear is not a particularly effective stimulus for my creative juices.

Still, as warm spring weather arrives, I develop a rhythm. The senior center offers an online exercise class three mornings a week, and I surprise myself by sticking with it. I start playing pickleball again, outdoors.

I sign a contract for 12 new windows for the sunroom, an expensive project that will take several weeks, but it gets me sanding and staining window ledges throughout the house. I set out lawn chairs, spaced at least six feet apart, and entertain friends for coffee.

Against all odds, I become adept at Zoom.

I cook. Chopped chicken liver — two kinds, a quick elegant liver paté and a traditional Jewish version with hard-boiled eggs and *schmaltz* (chicken fat) that matches my childhood memory. I experiment with poundcake recipes made with sugar substitutes, determined not to gain the "COVID 19."

I turn out pots of soups that last a week, get creative with beans, butternut squash, arugula, sausage, broccoli rabe. Whatever I make gets packed in containers and shared with neighbors.

When the reality hits that this isn't ending any time soon, I return to the studio. Several paintings are accepted for virtual art shows. In the past, book club friends would join me for the show and dinner. Not now.

I clean out drawers and cupboards and discover a trove of old garden magazines. I spend hours cutting out photographs and decoupage large bowls as gifts for friends and neighbors.

I spend hours in the garden, pruning, transplanting, thinning. Maybe install a firepit near the pond?

After almost a year of confinement, the house has never been this clean. I make my bed every morning, wash the same few dishes and put them away after each meal. I sweep and dust. I paint a guest bathroom, using the leftover red color from the front hall. It takes six hours and is very satisfying.

I read voraciously; a jigsaw puzzle is always in process. I could have used all this idle time to learn a new language — by now I could have become fluent in Italian. There is still time, the pandemic is still here. Instead, I paint and write.

Is this how prisoners survive? Finding ritual in routine, tiny triumphs in each day? Or do they go mad with the solitude? I look for things to fill the days; it would be easy to give in to the depression and loneliness. To give up.

I cannot do that. On the holiest of days in Judaism, Yom Kippur, the Day of Atonement, we fast for 24 hours. Except if you have a life-threatening illness; then it is forbidden to fast. You must eat — and live. It is the highest value, it is why when we toast, we say, Le'Chaim! To life! To waste this time we have on earth, pandemic or not, is the worst sin.

The holidays pass. No parties, no celebrations. Now it is winter, and there's no visiting with others, not even outside. When will this end?

This deep isolation has affected everyone. The feeling of loss is profound for the young; after all, a year is a huge percentage of their lives. For me, it is nothing, a blink of an eye. But I'm 80 now, I have a finite number of years remaining. To have lost a whole year not watching my granddaughters grow, that's painful.

Is this how I will die? As a COVID statistic? All the research shows the disease is morphing into a killer of old people.

I'm gonna die of something, why not this?

Saint Augustine prayed to God to "make him chaste, just not yet." I can relate. I'm certainly old enough to die without anyone being shocked and saying it was untimely. Let's face it, with each passing day the trajectory of my decline gets steeper. The loss of my cast-iron stomach, the lapses in memory, the aching joints will only get worse, and new ailments and afflications will come, for sure.

I expect I will die alone. Well, everyone does that ultimately. If someone is there with me, I hope I can muster up a decent last joke.

# I Want a Machete

**B**ut where do I buy one? I ask because I couldn't find one in Home Depot. Maybe Walmart? The plants in my yard are getting taller, wilder, and encroaching far beyond the areas where I put them.

Then there are the weeds. They are growing faster and bigger than I ever imagined. Not sure if it's global warming, the pandemic, or just my general inattentiveness.

I once watched a man in Hartford build an entire set of outside stairs with just a machete. Neighbors swear by their yard guy, a South American (Ecuador? Guatemala?), who arrives with machete in hand and swiftly reduces their tangle of small trees, vines, and overgrowth to a cleared space.

Of course, the reality is that if I had such a useful tool, I'd be more likely to sever a limb; mine, not a branch. My gardening tool of choice is a Ryobi recip-rocating saw. It's not too heavy for me to wield, and when I put it down, its bright chartreuse color tells me where I left it.

My husband David introduced me to this clever device. When I would ask him to cut something down in the garden, he brought out his battery-pow-ered Milwaukee Sawzall, a monster of a tool. He disdained garden loppers (designed for such tasks) as slow and inefficient.

I have the loppers but not the upper arm strength to use them on any branch over a half-inch thick. So I use the lightweight version of his Sawzall.

But I still imagine me with a machete. I love the idea of cutting the way through my jungle, slashing and chopping, no buttons to push, no trigger to pull, no motor noise, just the swish of the blade as it attacks and destroys ... Macha Machete Girl!

Fantasy, for sure, but a girl can dream.

# It's Just a Game

That's what people tell me about pickleball. It's fun, it's about the camaraderie, it's a great way to get much needed exercise.

Not to me. Sure, it's all that, but for me it's about staying relevant. I have given up so much, so many activities where I had a leadership role because I can no longer multitask, juggle six different things and complete them all successfully, and on time. Continuing to play a sport that I enjoy and am pretty good at was so very satisfying when I began eight years ago.

Fast forward and I still play several times a week. But I'm not the player I was then. My reaction time is slower, my stamina is less: I can play fewer consecutive games, my shots are not as hard.

And the culture itself has changed. Sometimes we could only get eight players to come out and we'd rotate partners. Now 30 to 40 people sign up. There are courts and tournaments in every town, and the players are all much younger, sometimes more than half my age. It's not a hard game to learn and many of the new players get good very quickly.

And yet I still play and play to win. My competitive instinct, honed by my older sisters, who showed no mercy and drove me to be better and try harder, is still alive.

I take pleasure in coaching new players. There are "beginner's nights," but no instructors, so I spend most of my time watching, helping, and encouraging new players. The sooner they are better, the more fun it will be to play with them. It's not that hard a game to learn; some will soon surpass me.

The average age today of players is 34.8. I am a dinosaur.

But while I can, I continue to play, for how much longer, I have no idea. Something will happen—a fall, an injury, a hip, an elbow, something will go wrong, and I will be sidelined, maybe forever. But for now, game on!

# *To Whom It May Concern*

Can I be good without God?

For some time now, I've realized that I don't believe there is an omnipotent, omniscient, and all-loving being, a Creator of the Universe. It's taken me a while, but nope, I don't believe.

The second question: can I call myself a Jew if I'm a non-believer?

There have been a few well-intentioned efforts to join the community of my fellow Jews. I went to a Yom Kippur service at a nearby synagogue when we lived in Illinois to say the Kaddish for my father. A Friday evening in a neighboring town's reform (meaning contemporary) service felt too frivolous, Judaism-lite. The tiny temple in the town where I live doesn't hold regular services, and other than painting their ceiling with clouds, I stay away.

Then there's the whole tricky business of an afterlife. I was once asked (rudely) by an acquaintance, how I could go on living if I do not believe in an afterlife. To this person, my lack of belief meant that I was condemned to hell at worst, and that at best, my life has absolutely no purpose.

It seems to me (and I believe it has been debated often by theologians with much more skin in the game) that the existence of a heaven or a hell is not dependent on my particular belief. It either exists or it doesn't. To say otherwise is to believe in fairies; if I say no, then Tinker Bell dies.

As no one living has any proof of its existence and being of a rational turn of mind, I can and do choose not to believe. But to say that therefore I will not be able to enter this "maybe yes and maybe no" place, or that my life has no meaning, makes even less sense. And why should I care? The wonder and miracle of being alive is not enough, there's something better later? I don't think so.

And what exactly qualifies one for entry into this Paradise? I flunked the first part: I don't believe it exists. But what if I did (or said I did ... does a well-told lie get me a pass?)? Wouldn't that be a cool surprise? Last laugh on me.

Does it matter that I'm Jewish? Is a Jewish afterlife different from a Christian, Buddhist, or Muslim one? The only possible benefit of such a place would be I'd see David again. But there would be all those other souls. I'm not good with crowds.

I choose to believe in nothing. That leaves a huge void about what comes next, but it also means that this is all I have, I can't count on salvation in some future time. It's now or never.

This earth, this time, this day, this life. I am trying to treasure it, to be the kinder, nicer being, to be the person you-who-doesn't-exist created me to be. If I believed in one, I don't think that God would care whether I fall to my knees five times a day, or that I cross myself and go to church on Sundays, or welcome the Sabbath by praising him and lighting candles on Friday nights.

The God I imagine cares little about the rituals and would rather I show my appreciation by doing good, not talking about it. On the contrary, I believe that if there is a God, then surely, he weeps at what we do to each other.

So, to whom it may concern: I'm giving non-believing a shot and I will see if, as the humanists say, I can be good without God. Wish me luck.

# Country Living

I am a stone-cold killer.

That reality struck home this morning as I drowned a red squirrel in my pond, in the Havahart device that caught him; an irony not lost on me. His last meal, peanut butter.

Perhaps it was a female, a mother, with a nest of babies waiting to be fed; they will probably now die. That trap has caught other creatures — small birds, an occasional gray squirrel. Those I release, as they don't chew on my house.

I had considered pinning the carcass, legs splayed, to the side of the garage, as a warning to others. Perhaps a row of them would show I meant business. Too ghoulish — children visit here.

What else? I attack spiders with a rolled-up magazine and a swift thwack (selectively, never daddy longlegs), and house flies. So many flies! Is it because there's a dairy farm just up the road? For those I have a choice of two fly swatters, hanging on a hook in my pantry.

Once I found a baby garter snake curled up on my basement floor. I set a gallon can of paint on top of him and left it there for a year. When I eventually removed the can, only a shriveled skinny swirl remained.

Mostly, I battle mice. The house is more than 100 years old, with a stone foundation; it has mice.

This was one household chore I could not delegate to my husband. As a boy in summer camp, David had learned to shoot a BB rifle, and became quite the marksman, once actually killing a bird in flight. He was so remorseful, he vowed never again and kept his word.

Instead, he practiced "catch and release," setting humane mouse traps and freeing the captured animals at the back of the yard or tossing them over the stonewall. Of course, they returned, and we went through the whole ordeal again.

Now I use poison.

A friend fills her bird feeder with high-quality seeds and nuts, food fit for human consumption. It attracts chipmunks, bird of all kinds, and gray squirrels. She resents the squirrels (and the hawk who waits patiently in a neighboring tree overseeing this smorgasbord), yet loves the chipmunks. I point out to no avail that while the cuteness quotient may be different, they are both rodents — and nuisances. She'd probably love my red squirrels.

As I sit typing in my office, a mockingbird leaps from the shadblow tree outside and slams into my window, its wings and beak hammering the glass before it returns to the tree. It does this several times before it flies away. It's been happening for weeks now. Is it seeing its reflection in the glass? Suicidal? Trying to tell me something?

Last summer my corgi discovered something under my car that got him barking and whining until I put him in the house. Getting down on the ground and peering, I saw the silhouette of a rabbit.

I went inside, got my keys, and slowly backed the car down the driveway, expecting the hare to hop away. He didn't move. He was alive, but barely, his entire back an open wound where a wide swath of flesh and fur were gone.

What could cause such a horrific injury? Had he been attacked by a hawk? What to do? He was clearly dying; I needed to put him out of his misery ... but how? Run him over with my car? Bash in his head with a rock or board?

I couldn't do it.

Instead, I shoveled his body up and dumped him at the edge of a neighbor's woods. "Let nature take its course." Sensible? Cowardly? Probably both.

Guilt, pity, righteous indignation, I felt all of that. You think living in the country is genteel? Trust me ... It's a killing field.

# Lost and Found

What has happened to my behind? What was once high, firm, and round, has become a deflated version of its glorious past. I used to joke that "you could crack an egg on my ass." Not anymore.

The aging body is not pretty. It's not just me. Old men's pants sag off their rears, their arms stick out from shirtsleeves as stringy sinews, not the rippling muscles of their prime.

The wrinkles and excess skin are everywhere, at the mercy of gravity. There is no question that a nip and tuck would do wonders, but once started, where to stop?

I once met Lillian Vernon, president of the eponymously named catalog, which sold everything unnecessary that you could want for your home.

She must have been in her early 80s. Impeccably dressed in a Chanel suit, makeup expertly applied, hair perfectly coiffed and colored, she looked fabulous. But her hands told a different story — they were the wrinkled, heavily veined, brown-spotted claws of an old woman.

Along with my butt, vanity has gone. I used to jest, "grown men weep at the sight of me." Today, I look better clothed than naked.

Long ago, a Frenchwoman told me that in growing old, "you must choose between your body and your face. You cannot have both," Of course, nowadays between scalpel and laser, one probably can. But why?

No matter what I do or don't do, no matter how much money I choose to spend, the fact is, it's a downhill trajectory, and the slope gets steeper every year. It's cheaper to accept the reality of the physical decline and just get on with my life.

Besides the loss of looks, the threat of Alzheimer's is always there, hovering over my shoulder and of much greater import. Since 2014, I've been a volunteer in a study of that most-feared disease, testing out a potential drug to delay the ravages of a declining brain.

No Botox for me. Instead, I've driven to New Haven monthly to receive an infusion in my arm, not knowing if it is placebo or drug. The nurses who manage my injections are delightful and caring, we are old buddies. Periodically, I am poked, prodded, and questioned to test my mental acuity. As I write this, after 64 doses over five-plus years, I am now receiving the actual drug.

Is it helping? I can't tell. After all, at 80, signs that appear to be incipient dementia could just be old age. Odd fragments from my far-away past randomly pop into my head, but where is my cellphone, or what did I go upstairs to find? These blank spaces are a daily occurrence. This morning, I spent 25 minutes searching for a missing paring knife which, it turns out, wasn't even in the kitchen but in yesterday's garbage at the bottom of the trash bin.

And forget about names. Yes, the years of mask-wearing definitely made recognition more difficult. But even without them, I have trouble remembering the names of people, including those I know well. When will I no longer recognize my children?

For now, it's just forgetfulness. But it will get worse. The question is whether my brain will last as long as my body. I'd prefer to die before I become senile, but unless I take matters into my own hands, it's a crapshoot as to which goes first.

The most painful part is having no older family members to ask, "do you remember ... ?" Everyone who knew me as a child is gone. My sisters, my cousins; the only relatives that remain are all younger than I. I have become the family matriarch, a lonely place and a role I feel inadequate to fill.

Meanwhile, I soldier on.

On the plus side, I am unleashed. Some might argue that my filters have always been paper thin, but now, what comes into my brain comes out of my mouth with barely a second's hesitation.

I have always suffered fools poorly, and now I simply let it rip. That alone is liberating. Am I an embarrassment to my children? Not yet — that may still happen.

Long ago, when I was living abroad, my father wrote me a letter after the sudden death of a young Israeli cousin I had a crush on. In it, he quoted Dylan Thomas:

"Do not go gentle into that good night,
Old age should burn and rave at close of day;
Rage, rage, against the dying of the light."

I wonder now why he chose to send that poem. My cousin and I were both young, in our 20s, my father was barely 50. Did he have a premonition of his own early death? I took it to mean that it was okay to be angry at the untimeliness of the death.

When it's my time, I will be a raging fire.

# *Vanity*

Observing the ravages of time on my body, I accept with equanimity most losses as the natural consequences of getting older: a wrinkle here, a sagging there. But then comes a specific blow that changes the calculus, that stops me in my tracks.

For me, it's my nose.

It's not a pretty picture. Ignoring the fact that everyone's nose, along with one's ears, grow larger as we age, this latest episode is the result of several surgeries that began a year ago to remedy a basal cell carcinoma in the middle of my nose (the follies of youthful, excessive tanning having finally caught up with me).

I have come to realize there is no Dorian Gray portrait of me aging in the attic. Instead, it's happening in the here and now. I am the loser in a cosmic bar brawl.

I am not alone in resisting the fact of my mortality.

A woman with graceful, long-fingered hands develops a cancer that leads to an amputated digit. A man takes pride in his capacity to work around the clock and is stricken with severe anemia. An opera buff loses his hearing, a political zealot who feeds on the written word goes blind.

Joan Rivers and the Duchess of Windsor refused to "age gracefully," and both died while undergoing still more plastic surgery. Houdini drowned in a freak accident while trying to prove his mastery as an escape artist. And of course, all those people who either didn't believe COVID-19 was real or pooh-poohed the reality of their vulnerability. Some, to their ultimate regret.

Why do we choose ignorance? Is it hubris or plain old vanity? Are we so caught up in the now that we completely ignore what lies ahead? We see old people hunched over, with walkers, and think "not me!" As the old joke says, "Denial is a river in Egypt."

For more than 40 years, I paid little attention to my physical body. Sure, I fretted about my weight, continually worrying about an extra five to 10 pounds, but basically, I ignored what I looked like.

What I experience now is a mirror of my early teens. Then, I obsessed over a zit on my chin. Now it's all these sudden wrinkles and skin tags — where did they come from? It feels like the same anxieties of youth are back again.

I don't want to be the last one standing, to outlive everyone I love. So why do I assiduously avoid behaviors that will shorten my life, like smoking, heavy drinking, eating with abandon?

Millennials know more about smoking, diet, and exercise and their consequences, but do they really think they will defy death? The other delusion is the notion that we will be exactly the same in 20 or 30 years — just with more gray hair.

I am just as guilty, assuming I will continue as I am until ... what? I drop dead while shoveling snow? Or suffer a stroke lugging my trash down the stairs?

But what if I don't die at a ripe old age, and instead become incapacitated, unable to speak, wipe my ass, feed myself? What about going blind? That would be a real game changer. I dread that more than a sudden demise at any age.

Control. I want some say as to how and when I leave this life. What could be more naive or arrogant? And yet ... I think about it a lot. Could I starve to death? Theoretically yes, but as I can't seem to lose the five pounds that have made a home in my belly, not eating at all seems unlikely.

The way we die isn't like in the movies. In my limited experience, it's ugly, and either much swifter or agonizingly slower than we wish. The best I can do now is rise each day to do battle, pen my obit — so I don't come off as a simpering saint, or doddering fool — and purge my house of useless memorabilia and anything that might embarrass my children.

I am flattered when people exclaim, "you don't look your age!"

Sure, my posture and foul mouth give the appearance of a younger Judy, but my body knows better. I am the Surfside condo, looking good on the outside, a crumbling hulk within. What will it be? A mole that doesn't heal? A pain in my side, a persistent cough?

Death is watching me, circling, waiting for an opening.

# *On My Mind*

The greatest gift David gave me was to make me feel competent. He believed in me and convinced me that I have good judgment and a nimble brain.

I pat myself on the back when I fix something. For me, it is a fresh experience. If on the rare occasion when I would question whether he could do something (install a skylight, rewire the entire house, build a pond), he would say, "Judy ... look at the people who do this?" meaning plumbers, mechanics, people who repair things.

Did I not believe he was as capable as they were? He was right: he could make everything. I limited myself to those aspects of our life that he wasn't good at: the computer, anything to do with words (although his spelling improved markedly after he started playing simple word games on his Palm), design, color, dealing with people.

He thought I had many talents; I am discovering that I have even more. I need to hold on to that feeling of competence, carry it around with me. It gives me substance. I exist in the world and can manage it.

But for how long?

In 2014, I read in the local newspaper about the A4 study, a new, nationwide Alzheimer project. In Connecticut the study was managed by Yale University. They were looking for volunteers, and so I wrote them, "I am a 73-year-old widow, in good health. I work part-time, drive, work out at a gym, serve as an elected vice-chair of my town's planning and zoning commission and, at the moment, have all my marbles."

I went through multiple tests and interviews, and finally, the last step, a PET scan, which showed I had sufficient plaque in my brain to meet their criteria, and so was accepted into the study. A friend was furious at me for participating — why would I want to know what I now know: that I am likely to develop the Big A.

As I cannot un-ring that bell, I prefer to move on and not dwell on it. But it hovers on the edge of my consciousness.

I spend a lot of time inside my head, talking to myself. After all, it's either that or talking to the dog, who, while a perfectly attentive listener, doesn't hold up his end of the conversation. It's not just because of COVID, it's a function of growing old alone, something I never imagined. I thought David, gone now 15 years, was indomitable — how naïve was that.

Here's some of what skitters across my brain.

My car's brake linings are too thin; they are supposed to be 8mm and are only at 4mm. The lining of my uterus is at 8mm, and the doctor says it is too thick, he wants it at 4mm. Perhaps my OB/GYN should talk to my mechanic?

Can a woman and a man be friends, pals, hang out together? In my younger years, I found such close friendships only possible with gay men, who, not considering me at all to their taste, treated me like a person. (I remember once praising a friend for some clever thing he'd done. I texted, "You da man!" To which he replied, "Sometimes ...")

Of course, I was labeled a "fag hag," an insult, implying that I hung out with gay men because no straight man would want me. Now that I'm old, I do have male straight friends, but it's because I'm no longer a threat or object of desire for anyone.

I can't complain. As women age, we fade from sexual object to invisible. That's true for me as well, until I open my mouth. I remember a dear friend saying he fell in love with me the first time he heard me on the telephone at work, demanding of a hapless sales rep, "What the fuck do you think you're doing?"

My mother said I spoke French like a Marseilles sailor (I rolled my "Rs"), and I swear like one, too.

Why do I keep exercising? I do it faithfully, three times a week, one hour of cardio, weights, and balance. And the point is? To keep upright and above ground. But if I lose my mind, does that make any sense? Will I be a limber vegetable?

My mother-in-law, Sophie, a sweet, retired educator, developed dementia in old age. She remained as cheerful as ever, but she would repeat the same questions over and over. It frustrated my husband, made him snappish. Did he see his future in her behavior? He died before it came to that.

When I visited Sophie after he died, she would ask, "Where's David?" I told her he "coming tomorrow." What was the point of telling her he was dead? She would only cry, then forget, and ask again. My idea of hell.

People my age have bucket lists. They check off exotic travel destinations, have facelifts, divorce spouses, and pick younger mates. For me, it is enough that I rise each day to do battle. Besides, I feel in my prime, however brief this state may be. My painting is better than ever, I am healthier than I've been in years, I write almost daily and find the act of putting the words on paper deeply satisfying.

And yet, there's this sense of urgency, that I'm creeping out to the thin end of the branch and what lies ahead for me isn't pretty. Will I be felled by a stroke, like my mother, or my sister, Ruthi? Is it the zeitgeist, or am I just facing reality? After all, I'm on the edge of the life stage described as "old-old."

At some point before she died, my mother had saved a box with sleeping pills. My sister Eva found it and flushed them down the toilet. It was cruel, and unnecessary, as they were mostly crumbled, and probably not enough to have done the trick. I think it gave my mother some sense of control at the end of her life.

Doesn't everybody want that? I know I do.

# Memento Mori

Remember you will die.

That's what the Latin phrase means. It's meant to humble those who think that riches, fame, or power will insulate them from the inevitable.

Yesterday was spent sorting through boxes — and more boxes — of family photos. I threw out about 20 pictures. At this rate, working daily, I will be 100 before I finish; is this how I want to spend my remaining time? I should just throw them all out. But all those people made up the tapestry of my childhood; I cannot bear to part with them.

I am surrounded by objects that all have a story.

Why save them at all? Like the collections of paperweights, oil lamps, wind-up toys, and myriad beautiful objects in my home that no one wants, who will care about these images when I am gone? They won't even know who's in them.

And if I label them? What for? They are long dead and if they had children, they already have similar pictures; and if childless — who else remembers them now?

I used to go antiquing and bought beautiful old picture frames with photographs still in them. I always threw the photos away. Will someone do that to the images I still cling to?

When David died, I went through the house and threw out or gave away hundreds of items from our shared life. I need to do that again.

When my Aunt Fritzie left Florida to go live in California near her son, she told me to take whatever I wanted from her home. My husband really wanted her black glass tabletop on its blond wooden base. I remember that table, so much more elegant than our all-wood table; back in 1944, hers was in a photo spread in *Interiors* magazine.

We flew to Florida and rented a truck to drive the table and eight chairs back north. The only other item I took was a short, wooden-handled spatula from her kitchen; I use it every day.

Why is it so hard to let go? Of things, of life.

Remember you will die.

A vivid reminder that when I am gone, all that I was — cantankerous, funny, loyal, opinionated, clever, stubborn, and many more not-so-generous adjectives — will soon be forgotten.

These morbid reflections are not just based on sorting through old photos; the day also included a visit to an old friend whose spouse just died. I saw them together two weeks ago. Usually chatty and gregarious, the soon-to-be deceased was distant; smiling but not engaged. I think he was waiting to die. Not untimely, as he was in his ninth decade; but his spouse's grief is as strong, the loss as daunting, as when they were newlyweds.

Maybe it's even harder, as the other is woven so tightly into one's existence, you cannot remember a time without them.

My greatest fear is that I will lose my mind long before my body disintegrates. Not only will I not be able to communicate, but I will forget David, or I will not recognize my sons or anyone I love.

What does it mean to be "alive," and not be "here" to experience it? How do I put one foot in front of the other, and for how long?

I imagine the worst — the reality is that if and when I lose my marbles, it will only be a problem for others, not for me, as I will not know I am only a shadow of my former self.

My mother-in-law was happy in her senility; I don't imagine I will be as sanguine. To quote the comedian, Ricky Gervais, "When you are dead, you do not know you are dead. It's only painful and difficult for others. The same applies when you are stupid."

Isn't that the truth?

When you are gone, you are soon forgotten. I leave behind my paintings, these scribbles, souvenirs of a long and rich life, tangible remnants of me. But the me that is *me* — that will be gone.

I continue sorting photos, 1,000 more get shredded.

Printed in the USA
CPSIA information can be obtained
at www.ICGtesting.com
CBHW041243060324
5024CB00024B/1852

9 781735 125275